CAR BEAUTIFUL

A Complete Guide to a Shiny, Well-protected Car

Wherein great controversies are stirred
anew, many tricky chemical secrets are
divulged, evil dangers to automobiles
are avoided and product names are named.

by Henry Watts

Loki Publishing Company
849 Gary Avenue
Sunnyvale, California 94086
   (408) 245-4040

iii

Cleanliness is next to godliness

— The Talmud

Cleanliness is indeed next to godliness

— John Wesley

They say cleanliness is next to godliness, Mabel;
I say it is next to impossible.

— George Bernard Shaw

Men argue, nature acts

— Voltaire

Good quotes about cleaning cars are
impossible to find.

— Henry Watts

Preface

The serious trouble started when I became curious as to what
the detailer was doing to my new car. It was 1986 and I had
just bought my first ever new car. I had bought vans new, but
never cars. This car was also my first Porsche, a 911
convertible named Loki. For many obvious reasons I wanted to
keep it as clean and protected as possible. My previous two-
seater had been a 1958 Mercedes 300SL ragtop, and I had already
gotten a tremendous and painful taste of the effort it takes to
get a car back to like-new condition after someone has been
actively ignorant, or worse. I was completely determined to
keep this car in the best possible shape.

During this time I was a little longer on money than time. Not
being willing to let my lack of free time result in neglect of
the car, I engaged the services of a well-recommended and well
checked-out detailer. My self-protective curiosity led me to
sit down with him and completely review his entire cleaning and
protection activities. It wasn't that I was completely
ignorant of all the issues, as I had frequently made extra
money during high school washing and waxing cars and have
continued to pay reasonable attention to the products
available. It was more that, with a brand new car on my hands
I wanted to be sure that everything was done in the best
possible way.

It would have been much easier if I could have taken the
approach used by my graduate advisor. He had a pale green
Citroen that ran fine, didn't have too many miles on it, but
only got washed when it rained in LA. His analysis was very
simple. The only reason for the paint was to protect the steel
from rusting. If the paint is good it will last for many years
with no care. When the paint wears out you simply have the car
painted (no doubt at one of the $39.95-for-a-complete-paint-job
shops then popular in Los Angeles). It's not clear why he
didn't just cover the car in Cosmoline; perhaps that involved
too much unnecessary work? If you are in total agreement with
McWhinney's approach this might not be the exact book for which
you were looking.

My curiosity began what turned out to be a quite lengthy process. After talking to several detailers, some body shops, several people active in concours and many manufacturers of car-care products, I can confidently report that there is only a limited amount of agreement on how to clean and protect a car. There were definitely times when I was quite sorry I had been so curious. It seemed like, while playing Monopoly, I had drawn a card from CHANCE that said, "You are going into a swamp and you will not be out for awhile." Now that the worst is over — not that my learning process on this topic is anywhere near completion — I am happy to share the information and biases that I have developed.

One conclusion does seems firm: to be sure that our cars are properly cared for we either have to to it ourselves or find a very special detailer. To be able to do it ourselves, however, we must sort through a great deal of information before we can be sure that we have the best available methods.

It really is fairly simple and quick to keep the car clean and protected. Much of the reason for the length of this book is not because the car care is so difficult, but rather to clarify some deep confusions so that the work can proceed simply. The book covers cleaning and protecting the exterior and interior of the car. Also included are lists and sources of supplies as well as cleaning checklists. If, after reading this book, all of this seems like too much work, there is still hope for the car. With the knowledge you have gained you should now be able to do a much better job of finding a detailer that you can trust with your car. You will know the right questions to ask, and you will know what to expect of the work the detailer does.

This book is written for people who wish to take good care of their cars but might be a bit baffled by all of the interesting and conflicting claims made by various people trying to sell us goods and services or who are just offering advice. My goal has been to find a reasonable balance between neglect and fanatical cleanliness. I have no quarrel with those who enjoy the process of cleaning their car and are perfectly willing to spend hours and hours achieving just a little bit more cleanliness and protection, or achieving it more often, but I am not one of those people. Included here you will find what I

believe to be an adequate amount of cleaning and protection
that also can be done with the least possible effort. Where
possible I have avoided esoteric 'tricks of the trade'. There
are many ways to get things clean. In each case I have
searched for the safest, most effective method, preferably
using materials that are easily obtained. When people tell you
that they know another way, not covered here, they may well be
correct. You will need to assure yourself that the proposed
method is sufficiently safe and effective.

This book is for cars that are in fundamentally sound shape, do
not need restoration, and are driven daily. Restoration is a
completely different topic and much too large to cover properly
in less than three or four volumes. Cars that are frequently
driven will generate more problems, or perhaps we should say
more challenges and opportunities, than cars that spend most of
their time in the garage under a cover.

There are lots of opinions in this book; some are very strong
opinions. Opinions are necessary in this field because we do
not have sufficient facts on which to base solid conclusions.
It may be that there exists a body of knowledge that could
clearly show us the very best approach for every cleaning and
protection problem, taking fully into account the basic nature
of the car, its current condition and the type of use to which
it is normally subjected. It is certain that no such body of
knowledge is currently available to the general public. Until
that time, the best we can do is act on the facts that we have
at hand, filling in the spaces with reasonably formulated
opinions. I am eager for reader feedback that will show better
ways of doing this important work.

I also suspect that some of the more diligent engineering
departments at companies like Meguiar's, Blue Coral, Turtle
Wax, Polyglycoat and the like have done some good research and
some good testing. I would issue them the following challenge:
send me the data. Do not send it via the marketing department.
Show the testing conditions (original state of the paint,
leather, rubber, whatever) and the results. Indicate the
amount of effort that each product required. Show your
products tested against each other as well as against the
competition. Indicate how you judge how long surface

protection lasts. If you do this I will publish your data in the next edition of this book.

This book started out as a series of articles for a small chapter of the Porsche Club of America. As it expanded, the scope was expanded slightly to encompass any car worth serious care. For the Porsche owners among you I have left in the specialized information that relates only to Porsches (swinging forward the mirrors during washing, for example).

A word about organization: This book follows the basic sequence that you might use to completely clean and protect your car. After the introductory chapter there are chapters on cleaning the exterior, protecting the exterior, cleaning the interior and protecting the interior. One final chapter wraps things up. Products are specifically named. Appendices II and III are a basic list and a complete list, respectively, of exact product names, approximate prices and where to get them. For products that are available by mail order, the names, addresses and phone numbers of various mail-order suppliers are listed in Appendix IV.

I would like to thank all those people who provided help in preparing this book. Much of the information is from them, though they are not, of course, responsible for any errors or anything that gets me into extended disagreements about the theology of car care. Not one of them totally agrees with everything written here, nor do they totally agree with each other. While several people have reviewed the writing, and several manufacturers have been patient enough to share long telephone conversations, it must be noted that, without the detailed, gracious, voluminous and expert input of Chuck Davis, Steve Douglas, Brian Perry, and David Wong, all from Zone 7 of the Porsche Club of America, none of this would have been worth printing. Jeff Stern of Meguiar's, Jay Kolinsky of Malm's and Dr. Les Legosi of Classic all provided useful input. I also owe a debt of thanks to Penny Brisson, the editor of the Loma Prieta Region (Zone 7) newsletter. She provided the original inspiration and publishing opportunity that helped all this become a book.

A. PRINCIPLES AND SUPPLIES

You are going to need to throw away your chamois, your wool
wash mitt, your washing sponge, and maybe the soap you use to
wash your car. If you don't want to use any silicones on your
rubber you'll also need to trash your Armor All, Clean Eze and
Meguiar's Formula 42. Even if you knew all of that already,
there may still be some useful information for you here.

1. Good Car Care Information is Difficult to Find

There does not, until this book, seem to be a simple and
accurate way to find the best way to take very good care of
your car. There are wildly contradictory claims running about.
There is bad literature. There are manufacturers who sell
excellent and very dangerous products side by side. And there
are experts on nearly every side of every question.

A search for good information has led me to discussions with
head chemists of companies making products for car care,
marketing departments, heads of small companies. It has also
unearthed some interesting controversies. These include wax
selection, rubber care products and the choice of washing
soaps. Through all of this I have been desperately trying to
stay away from a scientific approach which would involve long-
term tests of all of these products. So far I have succeeded.
It is tempting, however, to put some of the claims I have heard
to serious test. I think this would, unfortunately, require a
great deal of time and energy over several years' time.

In the literature search I have been able to do thus far I have
not turned up anything that I would consider to be of real use.
One book was recommended to me. Given what I have to say about
it I think I should not name it. It is available through
various automotive book catalog stores. Reading this book was
a most interesting experience. The book is basically oriented
toward cleaning up your disasterously neglected '72 Dodge
Duster. The book suggests, among other things, that taking
decals off paint (God forbid!) can be done with a razor paint

scraper carefully used(? !!!), that paint thinner can be used to remove road tar, that clear lacquer should be sprayed about the engine compartment on just about everything (hoses, over any engine paint, on the intake manifold, any rubber parts, air cleaner, et cetera, ad nauseum) and nowhere mentions anything about cleaning or protecting leather. While these approaches may be reasonable for an older, very rough-shape car that will never have any real value, they are downright dangerous (at least financially) for cars that do have real value. My copy of this other book is available to the first person who asks, but only if they promise to use it as kindling in their fireplace.

2. The Problems to be Solved

The problems we are trying to solve in cleaning the car are generated in three way. Things get dirty, things get damaged and things deteriorate on their own. It follows that we have to be able to clean (without doing damage), do minor repair and refresh or reinvigorate those things that are trying to deteriorate on their own.

These categories are not mutually exclusive. Abrasive dirt leads to deterioration as the dirt is pushed around the paint's surface by the wind, by your car cover or by the mitt you use to wash the car. Or it can lead to the grinding away of your carpet, if that is where it is embedded, as you tap your feet to the tunes of your favorite bluegrass group. (I suppose that if you listen only to Mantovani, never tap your feed, and are exceptionally careful getting into and out of the car, you may be able to vacuum less often. But you will still need to vacuum.) Bugs splattered on the front of your car also lead to deterioration. Their poor little bodies are quite acidic, and they tend to eat away the paint until they are washed off. Bird droppings are also acidic, causing similar problems. Nor is even the fine dirt film as inert and unchanging as it appears to be. Scientific tests have demonstrated that dirt that falls onto a surface can, at first, be blown off. After two or three days, however, the dirt/dust has somehow become bonded to the surface, requiring washing and perhaps scrubbing.

The category of things deteriorating includes anything you can smell. The reason that you can smell new leather and the reason that leather left unattended will harden and deteriorate are partially the same reason: in this case, oils are evaporating. Other things deteriorate in sunlight or in the presence of oxygen. It is a nasty perspective, realizing that many key parts of our precious cars are, even as they sit, accumulating dirt and deteriorating. Life is like that sometimes. Still, there is much that we can do.

In addition to cleaning the car and doing minor repair and rejuvenation as needed, we also want to take whatever reasonable steps we can to protect the car; we want to slow the deterioration process and keep the dirt that will be coming our way from getting too firmly attached to the car or into places where it will cause a lot of damage.

3. The Benefits of Cleaning the Car

Doing this work which, on the surface, as it were, looks like drudgery, has many special benefits in addition to cleaning and protecting the car. It can be a mystical experience simply to observe, firsthand, the process of a car shedding its dirt and beginning to look, once again, like the proud Teutonic (Italian, American, Japanese, British) creation it truly is. Layer by layer the dirt peals off and the true soul emerges.

There are benefits to you, of course, since you get to drive around in such a clean and spiffy-looking car. This is not all vanity. A few years ago National Semiconductor filmed a marvelous documentary about four of their employees visiting a factory in Japan, better to understand how the Japanese workers achieve their impressive productivity. The film showed the four Americans touring the factories, shopping at an electronics supermarket, having dinner, all the while discussing various topics about the Japanese life style and the Japanese approach to work.

At one point during a walk down the street Glenn Frater, one of the two American men on the trip, was having his shoes shined by a middle-aged man who was plying his trade among the sidewalk foot traffic. Glenn was being pushy in a friendly way. He asked the shoeshine man, through the interpreter, whether he liked his job. The man said yes, that it was important work. Glenn pushed a little more, and asked if the man didn't think it demeaning to be shining shoes. The man, with his face showing dignity and a little amusement, looked directly at Glenn and said, "If your feet are not right, you are not right."

For many of us our car is fully as personal as our shoes, and we will have a better perspective during our daily lives if the car we drive is well-maintained.

Another benefit is that you are able to stay well in touch with the current health of your car, seeing and fixing minor problems before they have the chance to become major. This being-in-touch (literally) is a natural and pleasant side effect of spending time working with essentially all the observable parts of the car. This state of being-in-touch with a machine is described in Robert Pirsig's book, "Zen and the Art of Motorcycle Maintenance". This excellent book, as it unfolds, turns out to be a lot more about craziness than Zen or motorcycles, but in the first fifty pages or so it offers a lovely perspective on the differences between being-in-touch with a machine, and simply riding or driving a machine that others maintain. He talks at length about how he does his own maintenance and therefore knows about his machine, while his friend, John Sutherland, simply rides his BMW and expects it to run between normally scheduled in-shop servicing. Vehicle chauvinists might note, however, that, to some extent Pirsig's attitude might be a result of Pirsig riding a British machine while John's motorcycle is a German-made BMW.

The work to be done is divided into four main chapters: cleaning the exterior, protecting the exterior, cleaning the interior and protecting the interior. There is some overlap, as there are rubber and painted parts both inside and outside the car. The engine compartment and the glass will be treated as part of the exterior.

___

4. A Minimalist Approach

The first and one of the more absolute principles of car care is that you do not use a stronger chemical than you need. One of the things that creates so much confusion about car care is that people discover that some procedure apparently works, but may not realize the damage that they may be doing. Detergents will clean leather. Lacquer thinner will remove tar (so will scouring pads and Ajax). One of our key objectives is to sort out what works from what doesn't, and then determine, among the things that work, which ones will do the least damage to the car. To make these decisions we will, throughout the book, have to get involved in understanding our enemy, the dirt.

5. Cloths & Bottles

Cotton is the cleaning material of choice. It is soft, reasonably absorbent and easily cleaned. Use a cotton wash mitt. Wool wash mitts should be avoided. The wool fibers are a little harsher than cotton, and will eventually add minor scratches to your paint. It will take some time for all of this to show up, but why do it the wrong way. It will show up sooner on cars with dark paint. Such scratching is one of the sources of spider webbing, which can be most easily seen when a dark car is viewed in full sunlight. Wool also tends to grab and retain the dirt particles, so you end up sanding the paint with the dirt embedded in the wash mitt. Not good. Nor should you use a sponge. The sponge does a great job of carrying a large amount of soapy water to the car's surface, but the dirt and grime it picks up tend to stay in the sponge. Note that cotton mitts will not carry quite as much soapy water to the car as will a wool mitt or a sponge, but you soon become used to slightly more frequent trips to the soap bucket.

Cotton, either in the form of diapers or terrycloth towels (100% cotton) should be used for drying the car. The classic chamois does a great job of absorbing the water, but, like wool, tends to trap the dirt. Some people also believe that the chamois tends to pull on the wax and remove some of it. Jay Kolinsky of Malm's disputes the notion that the chamois

will remove wax. In any case, my view is that you'd best put
that chamois away.

You will need diapers, if not for drying the car then for other
procedures later. If you end up buying new diapers (about $1
each at major toy or department stores) wash them two or three
times before attempting to use them. The manufacturers seem to
put some sort of starch in to help the cutting and sewing
processes, and the unwashed fibers are naturally a little
stiff. The best way to get the diapers is to get them used
from a diaper service. These companies usually sell the
diapers when they get a little old. You will get a diaper that
is well broken in, which is to your advantage. You will pay
about 30 cents each, about a third of the new cost. Get 50 or
so; otherwise you nearly have to do a rag laundry every time
you do any cleaning on the car. Be sure you know whether you
are buying the old, single-layer type of diaper, or the pre-
stitched kind. I prefer the single layer type as it allows me
to fold or unfold the diaper as much as is needed

A handy tool for applying many liquids is a spray bottle.
These are usually available at hardware stores. The 16 oz.
size works pretty well most of the time. Use these when you
end up buying chemicals in quart or gallon cans.

6. Emulsifiers

Another useful chemical tool is an emulsifier. An emulsifier,
in this context, makes petroleum products such as oil and
grease soluble in water. It is used as a degreaser and general
cleaner. Soap and detergent are, to a certain extent,
emulsifiers. When used in this book, however, the term
emulsifier refers to the super-concentrated products such as
Swipe, or products that can be used from the bottle, such as
Armor All Cleaner and Simple Green. Swipe is my favorite as it
is the cheapest and comes in a super-concentrated form. You
can then dilute to suit your purpose. Be sure not to use Swipe
at full strength unless you have a VERY SERIOUS dirt problem on
your hands (or on your car).

Emulsifiers seem to be the best choice for the engine compartment and under the wheel wells as they will generally not have very much effect on tar or undercoating. These products are alkaline and will also tend to remove the wax, though not with the immediate and total finality of a solvent, and they may not always be very gentle with the paint. The instructions with Swipe indicates that it can be used for wax stripping if used hot, at full strength and if it is left on for two minutes. Use all emulsifiers very judiciously on the painted surfaces and only if you are going to wax that section. You should also avoid using such alkaline products on aluminum and pot metal, as strong alkalis will etch these metals.

7. Solvents

Solvents, in this book, refers to petroleum products that will dissolve other petroleum products. If you can't tell from the label whether the cleaner in your hand is an emulsifier or a solvent, see if the ingredients refer to petroleum distillates. These are solvents. Solvents are also used as degreasers. These solvents will remove essentially all the wax on a car, so you should use them on the painted surfaces only if you intend to wax the car immediately. They will also tend to dissolve undercoating so you should not use such solvents in the wheel wells. They are best used when the temperature is on the warm side. The warmth helps them evaporate more quickly, minimizing the amount of time they are on the surface of your car. To the extent that cured paint still has oils in it, solvents will tend to remove these oils. This is not a serious problem for the uses that are indicated in this book, just something of which you should be aware.

No.7 Tar Remover is effective as a general solvent and is easily available in small containers from auto supply and parts stores. No.7 is the new brand name for most of the automotive care products that used to be sold under the DuPont label. Prepsol, a bodyshop wax and grease remover that is used as a pre-paint cleaner is also a reasonable choice and works quite well. These bodyshop products are designed to remove grease, oil, wax, anything but paint. Other brandname choices for products similar to Prepsol are are Cleans All, Acme 88-Klix,

Polysol and Grow's Super-Klean.   Read the labels carefully.
These products tend to slightly penetrate and soften the paint,
which is OK if you are going to paint the car, but is otherwise
no good at all.   One product that specifically indicates that
it softens paint is Grow's Super Klean.   It is likely that the
Grow's product is not substantially different from the others.
Grow's should probably get some extra credit for better
labeling than is found on most of these products. On the other
hand, I have a strong tendency to avoid any product that
explicitly threatens to soften the paint.

8. No Gasoline!

One of the things you will not find recommended here is the use
of gasoline to clean anything.   Gasoline belongs in your gas
tank and nowhere else.   It is true enough that gasoline will
work very effectively as a solvent, but it is very dangerous.
Just because they allow 16-year-old kids to pump the stuff
doesn't mean that it is inherently safe.   Gasoline also tends
to leave a greasy, resinous film. Gasoline vapors are heavier
than air and tend to stay around on the ground.   (It is the
fumes that burn, not the liquid.   Liquid gasoline is difficult
to ignite.   On a cold day you can put out a lighted match by
dipping it into liquid gasoline.   Take my word for this and DO
NOT TRY IT.)   If gasoline fumes reach a heater pilot light or
other source of ignition in the right concentration you are in
for one of the more thrilling experiences of what could become
your abruptly foreshortened life.   When we need serious
cleaning power we will turn to pre-paint cleaners or, as a last
resort, lacquer thinner.   Lacquer thinner is slightly more
civilized than gasoline; it too, is flammable, but it will tend
to burn your house down, not demolish it in one spectacular
explosion as gasoline can.   Because there are cases that
require very aggressive solvents you should attempt to buy all
your cleaning brushes with wooden handles.   Lacquer thinner
will dissolve many plastics including some plastic brush
handles. If you are still not convinced that you shouldn't use
gasoline for cleaning, read Appendix V and learn from Garry
Korpi's experience.

Anyone using solvents at home, including in the driveway, should have a fire extinguisher handy and know exactly where it is.

An additional safety note: Solvents, even when unlit, have been demonstrated to be damaging to people. Longterm exposure, even to light concentrations, has been shown to increase miscarriages and lead to respiratory problems.   Longterm overexposure has been demonstrated to cause permanent brain damage, according to the label on the Grow's Super-Klean. Don't breath any more of these solvents than you must, and put them away, tightly capped, as soon as you are able.

9. Brushes.

For almost all activities related to cleaning the inside or outside of a car, it is important that the brushes used be as soft as possible. Get natural bristles whenever possible. Dental research has indicated that teeth can be worn away by bristles that are too stiff, so it isn't surprising that stiff brushes will scratch your paint, plastic surfaces and soft metals.   As mentioned before, avoid plastic handles or even painted handles. Plain wooden handles are the best.

10. Read the Directions

Obviously is it the simplest of common sense to completely read the directions of any product that you bring anywhere near your car. This doesn't mean that you might not have occasion to use a product somewhat differently than the manufacturer had in mind, based on your own experience or recommendations from trusted friends. Nevertheless, the manufacturers are the ones who should know the most about the product. You should read what they have to say. Additionally, there are strong product liability reasons that encourage the manufacturer to divulge, on the product package, any dangers that the product might pose to you and/or your car.

You'll notice that, so far, we haven't actually talked about any work to be done. All you have invested in this exercise is some reading time. The key idea is to get the confusions straightened out so that the work can be made as easy as possible.

B. CLEANING THE EXTERIOR

11. Choosing a Soap

The first step in cleaning a car is washing it, but before beginning the washing we need to choose a soap. The objective for the soap is to emulsify the oil and grease (that is, change the oil and grease so that they can be dissolved in water), and reduce the surface tension so the the dirt will tend to float off.   The soap should also be able to be rinsed off without leaving a residue behind, not be abrasive, and, while doing all of this, not attack the wax. Avoid any powdered soaps. There is a chance that some of the particles will not dissolve; they then become grit that will scratch the surface.   This is probably a very small danger, but why take the chance when there are plenty of good car washing liquids available?

After listening to a great deal of discussion, I have concluded that the best approach is probably to use the commercially available car wash soaps. Meguiar's, Classic and Raindance all make acceptable products. One of the problems with testing the effectiveness of the soap is that the bad effects are likely to be on the wax.   All of the other products you might pick to wash the car will probably do a great job CLEANING the car. On the other hand, it is very difficult to tell, without extended experimentation,   exactly how much damage any one of these products will do to the wax.   How do you easily tell how much wax a soap has removed from your car?

Some people use liquid dishwashing soaps to wash their cars. These are strong detergents and some may be highly alkaline. Washing your car with these is a very bad idea.   Strong detergents will remove the wax on your car and may burn (oxidize, I think) the paint.   The difference between soap and detergent, by the way, is that soap is animal fat combined with an alkali (such as lye), whereas detergent is a petroleum product that has similar (but more powerful) capabilities. This is where we get the term 'soft soap'; soft soap contains a lot of lye.   Detergents will clean remarkably well.   I have seen industrial tests that indicate that Joy does a superb job, both in terms of doing the cleaning and being willing to be rinsed off with no remaining residue. And don't be fooled by the brand name of Liquid Ivory. While the Ivory bar soap is soap, the liquid is a detergent.

Other people have suggested liquid Woolite, and Johnson's Baby Shampoo. Mother's wisdom says that baby shampoo leaves a residue on baby's head and will probably leave you one on your car as well. The Woolite may be OK; at least I didn't find any strong counter arguments. It does like cold water.

I had a delightful conversation with Dr. Les Legosi, chief chemist for Classic car-care products. His view was that anything would be adequately safe if you were sure that it was only mildly alkaline. He suggested that Woolite and baby shampoo might be OK, but thought that those solutions would be more expensive than a commercial car washing product. He did not believe that, under the normal conditions for washing a car, any of these products would leave a residue, although we must keep in mind that using cold water to wash a car makes it more difficult to get all the soap residues off.

My choice is Meguiar's MG-00 Professional High-Tech Car Wash or Classic. The clincher for me is this: you can be sure that Woolite, Ivory, Joy, Johnson's Baby Shampoo etc. are NOT testing their product to make sure it will leave the nice carnuba wax on your car. Only car-oriented companies would do such testing. I think the car-soap controversy (baby shampoo & Woolite, indeed!) is really a matter of the concours afectionados getting a little carried away. In any case, do not use very much of whatever you select.

You might also wish to consider whether you need any soap at all. This will depend on whether you have done a good job keeping the car waxed, and on the amount and type of dirt on the car. Using no soap is the best way to leave the wax in good shape. However, the dirt that is on the car will not have the surface-tension-reducing benefits of the soap, and might tend to scratch the paint a bit more while you are washing the car. Also, some road film, which tends to be greasy in nature, is unlikely to come off with water, even if the car has an

excellent coat of wax on it.   I would suggest the following
rule: if the car is clean enough and waxed enough that you can
get it clean by just hosing it off (gently with the hose,
please) then you can get away with using no soap. On the other
hand, if you are going to have to swab around in order to get
the car clean, you should have some soap in your bucket.   I
think a good car-washing soap is not very hard on the wax, and
I am more fearful of the scratching, so I always use soap.

12. Getting Going

You may find, as you contemplate the work involved in properly
cleaning the car, that your mind wanders to other topics and
you continually put off doing this important task.   One trick
that I use, when various parts of my psyche are fighting over
what I should do, is to simply agree with myself to PREPARE to
do the needed job.   The preparation, in this case, involves
getting all the supplies ready and laid out efficiently so that
they will be well at hand while I am working.   Often I find
that, having gotten so far as to do the preparation, the work
itself doesn't seem like such a big deal, and I go ahead and do
it. Even if this doesn't happen, whenever I next have a little
bit of time I know that everything is ready for me to begin
immediately.

13. Where and When to Wash (and Wax)

Washing and waxing must be done in the shade, but there is more
to it than just that. First, when washing, a hot surface will
tend to evaporate off the water before you have a chance to dry
the surface. This will leave water spots. Many waxes will dry
up too quickly and to a super-hardened state if left to sit on
a hot surface.   The point is this: the car surface cannot be
hot.   This means that you can't drive your black car that has
been sitting in the summer noontime heat into a small patch of
shade and begin the cleaning. Also, watch out for the heat of
the engine cover if the car has just been driven. Work indoors
if you have good enough light.

I think that the best time to wash is late in the day, when the

sun is low enough to provide nice shade. The car is likely to
be cooler than in midday. Morning works well too, but in the
late afternoon the limited time available tends to keep me
focused on the work and I tend to finish quicker.

By the way, commercial car washes are OUT OUT OUT. The
brushing action is much too abrasive, the brushes are harsh,
the detergents may not be as mild as we would like, and
sometimes too much of the dirt, especially around the bottom of
the car gets taken off in the drying process. All of this
could leave you with a free afternoon but too many scratches on
your car. It may be that there are car washes that are safe,
but I have not seen one that I would use.

14. Proper Dress Code for Cleaning the Car

Be sure to remove rings and belt buckles when working on the
exterior of the car. It is all too easy, leaning over fenders
and such, to put a scratch in the paint. You can look spiffy,
with your buckle and rings, later, when the car looks spiffy
too. The proper song for cleaning the car, in case you thought
that there wasn't one, is the old standard "You Belong to Me."

15. Preparation for Washing

Occasionally, before washing the car, look at the underside of
the bottom of the doors to verify that the door drain holes are
open. If not, every washing and every rainy drive will leave
water standing in the bottom of the inside of the door, leading
to lots of rust as well as a damp moldy feeling and smell
inside of the car.

A special note for Porsche owners: the modern-style Porsche
side mirrors, which will pivot out of the way, tend to collect
water on the inside of the mirror housing, just under the lower
edge of the glass. To prevent this, rotate them toward the
front of the car. From this position they will drain much
better.

16. Preparing the Tough Areas

If you keep your car well waxed and wash it often, you will
find that dirt, grime, tar and other unpleasantnesses tend not
to stick to the surface. You can then read much of this book
with a quiet smile on your face, thinking of all the
"opportunities" you have avoided.

Hose off the car. Use a gentle setting on the hose nozzle at
first, or just use a plastic on/off nozzle. The on/off nozzle
will allow you to turn the water on and off, avoiding water
waste, and will provide a very gentle flow of water. You are
trying to get the surface wet, not blast the grit around the
surface. The dirt that does not come off with a gentle flow of
water is merely waiting for you to arrive with a soapy wash
mitt. While you are prepping the tough areas the water will be
loosening the dirt and bugs on the painted surfaces of the car.

This is also the right time to spray off the underside of the
car as well as you can. For this use a high-pressure nozzle.
Be sure you remove all of the mud caked on under the car. You
want to do this now so that this stuff doesn't splatter onto
the painted surfaces after you have gotten the outside of the
car clean. If you drive on salted roads is it even more
critical that you get the underside of the car completely
rinsed.

Spray your chosen emulsifier (1:1 Swipe) inside the wheel
wells, under the motor, inside the motor compartment, through
the engine cover screen, along the rocker panels and on the
lower edge of the front spoiler. Put it on the wheels only if
they are chrome. Try to keep this off of paint as it will have
a slight tendency to remove wax.

Inside the motor compartment you might also use a product
called Gunk. Gunk is a fairly strong solvent (they call it a
self-emulsifying degreaser, but it is solvent, not alkali).
This used to be an excellent product for general engine
cleaning, and is still good for cleaning mechanical parts.
However, the warnings indicate that it will remove wax, may
streak the paint and is bad for plastic. Most modern cars have
important plastic parts under the hood, so I would think that

the use of Gunk should be left to cleaning greasy car parts.
It is very good for cleaning motorcycles (which is actually
much more difficult than cleaning a car) as long as you keep it
off the plastic and paint.

Hose off all the areas where the emulsifier has been sprayed.
True fanatics will scrub out the wheel wells. Have fun if this
is your choice too. In all these areas except under the engine
cover you can use a fairly high-pressure setting on your
nozzle. Around the engine be sure to maintain some respect for
the air-intake areas of the motor and all electronics. Avoid
direct water spray on the secondary fuse box that is sometimes
found in the engine compartment and on the distributor. Steam
cleaning of the engine will also hasten the failure of the
fuses as well as endangering other electronics.

Wipe down the inside of the hood and trunk lid with a solvent
(No.7 bug & tar remover or Prepsol). Clean well around the
battery, as this area will tend, over time, to corrode. Any
rags used to clean around the battery should be put immediately
into the rags-ready-to-be-washed bin. The white stuff you are
wiping off is composed of salts of hydrochloric acid and these
will attack just about anything they touch. If the battery
connections are not protected grease them or spray with
Permatex Battery Protector.

17. Cleaning Chrome

Before washing is also a good time to deal with any chrome trim
on the car. You need to be sure you can tell the chrome from
the aluminum. Not all of the bright metal trim on modern or
older cars is chrome. Aluminum is often used to reduce weight
and many side trim pieces are simply polished aluminum. Chrome
is much shinier and looks very smooth and hard. Aluminum has a
duller sheen and is a much softer surface. If you are unsure
of the difference, ask someone who knows before proceeding.
The discussion of chrome and aluminum will ultimately involve
the care of wheels; wheel care will be covered in the very next
section.

To care for aluminum that is polished (shiny) but does not have

a surface coating (gold, black, clear) use Happich's Simichrome
(German product, therefore the strange spelling).   Simichrome
is a medium polish, and will bring weathered aluminum to a nice
sheen.

The chrome parts will enjoy a stiffer cleaning. IF AND ONLY IF
you are going to wax the chrome, you need to look, before you
wash the car to see if any of the chrome needs a little
freshening up. Chrome corrodes fairly easily as it is actually
a porous material, allowing moisture and chemicals to penetrate
to the metal underneath.   If your chrome is a little corroded
it can be brought back to good luster with the use of VERY FINE
steel or brass wool (00 to 0000 guages).   Brass is preferable
as it is softer and the small bits of it that come off the pad
will not cause rusty spots wherever they happen to end up.   I
have heard that stainless-steel wool also exists, but I have
not been able to find it.   The brass should work fine.   This
should always be used with an emulsifier (30:1 Swipe) solution
or your solvent to soften the impact of the wool and help wash
away the grit and grime.   Rinse well, lest the shedding fibers
scratch the paint during the washing process. All this should
only be done before waxing; the porous chrome always needs a
good coat of wax over it.   Be sure not to use steel or brass
wool on aluminum.   The metal pads will severely scratch the
aluminum surface.

18. Cleaning the Wheels

How you clean your wheels will depend on what they are made of.
Wheels may be painted, chromed or alloy (aluminum).   Some of
the newer wheels (especially on Porsches) are an aluminum alloy
that has over it a clear anodization.   It is hard to see this
anodization, but it is very important to keep it in good shape.
Each type of wheel requires a different treatment.

Painted wheels, or wheels that have painted sections are cared
for as with any other painted surface, normal washing and
waxing.

Wheels that are unprotected aluminum can most effectively be
cleaned and polished with Happich's Simichrome.   It is OK to

use solvents to clean dirty aluminum wheels before using the Simichrome. Do not use alkali (emulsifier) products on unprotected aluminum.

Chrome wheels get the same treatment described in the preceding section for other chrome parts.

To care for the newer wheels and any other aluminum parts that have a clear or a black anodization, use soap and water or solvents. Do not use any polish, metal wool or other abrasives on anodized aluminum. Alkaline products like Swipe are also not recommended as they probably can etch away the clear anodization. You want very much to leave the clear layer in place, especially on the wheels, as it provides very important protection. You can also use P21S wheel cleaner for cleaning alloy wheels that have clear anodization.

Another option for alloy wheels is the trendy approach of polishing them to a high gloss. I do not favor this because 1) I don't think it looks as good as the original factory dull sheen, and 2) if the wheels used to have a clear anodization coating, it now becomes much more critical to take special and frequent care of the unprotected aluminum. Working against the wheels is the brake dust from the brake pads. This dust is very acidic and will rapidly corrode the unprotected wheels. Nor does it seem that you can solve this problem easily by changing to the dustless brake pads. The ones I have tried either were very hard on the brake rotors, did a very poor job of stopping the car, or both.

Wheels are difficult to clean because of all the contours and features. One of the more effective ways of cleaning the wheels is to let whatever chemical you have applied do its job, then use a 4" paint brush and a swirling or jamming motion to clean the wheels and scrub them out. This is a gentle treatment and will get into the various nooks and crannies quit well.

Rinse the car again.

19. Wash and Rinse the Car

Add a little soap (or don't; see section 11), then fill your
wash bucket with water and get the wash mitt soaking in the
soapy water.   No need to use excessive amounts of soap, that
just tends to attack the wax more than you wish.   Use just
enough soap to give some nice suds.   If it is cool out,   treat
yourself to warm water.   Work your way around the car with the
soapy mitt,   pausing often to clean it in the wash bucket,
squeezing it out and letting it soak up soap. Start at the top
of the car, then do the higher parts of the sides, then finally
the lower parts of the car where things will be the dirtiest.
This avoids picking up a lot of dirt in the mitt when cleaning
around the lower part of the car and using the dirt to sand the
top of the car.   Be sure to wash the door jambs and the edges
of the trunk and engine cover. You will need a small cloth for
this, and you will have to get the soap off by wiping down with
a very wet rag.

Use a straight motion when washing, drying, waxing and buffing.
Circular motions will tend to cause swirl marks.

Wash very carefully.   Whatever you do not find with the soapy
mitt you will inevitably find with your drying rag or the wax
applicator.   This isn't like doing dishes; (Dad, who always
washed, claimed that the person drying dishes was expected to
remove about a third of the food).   As you get good at washing
the car you can take pride in drying the car and ending up with
wet but perfectly clean diapers that you used for drying. This
does take some skill.   Dirt is a lot easier to see when it is
dry than when you are in the middle of doing the washing.

While you are washing it is a good idea to wash the outside of
the windows as well as the already-cleaned wheels.   Later you
will clean the windows with a special solution,   but that
process will work better if you have already gotten the worst
of the dirt off the glass.

The tops and rear windows of convertibles also need to be
washed.   How often will depend on the frequency with which the
tops are used.   The top can be washed with water or a mild
solution of Woolite, then rinsed very thoroughly.   Leave the

top up until it is completely dry, as stowing a damp top will
lead to mildew.

Rinse the car again, using a gentle spray but letting the water
flow, taking with it all the chemicals you have been using and
all the dirt that is now sitting loose on the car.   You might
wish to rinse each section of the car as you finish washing it.
This will help reduce water spotting.   It will depend on how
fast you work. If you are quick and the car is not very large,
a rinse at the end should be fine. If you are taking your time
washing, you should probably rinse as you go.

20. Miscellaneous Cleaning

Now that you have rinsed the car you have a dilemma.   You want
to dry the car immediately, because water spots will form if
the car dries itself (see section 26 for a discussion of water
spots).   However, you have some other cleaning work to do,
mostly getting any resistant tar, sap, big bugs, etc. off the
car.   When you get these special opportunities cleaned up you
will have to rinse and dry the car again. Drying the car twice
seems like unnecessary work, no?

The solution depends on the extent of the tar/sap/bugs. If
there is a great deal of tar, sap, or big bugs that have not
come off in the washing process, then you probably have to dry
the car, do the tar/sap/big-bug removal, rinse the parts where
you have been working and dry those parts.   However, if you
have just a little bit of work to do removing tar/sap/big-bugs,
then work quickly, very quickly, and all should be well.

There are apparently five basic ways of removing these
'opportunities'   from the surface of the car or parts in the
engine compartment.

First, the bugs will come off eventually if you just continue
to rub, very softly, with your wash mitt and some soapy water.

Secondly, we can dissolve the offending substances in a solvent.

The easiest solvent to obtain is a bug & tar remover such as No.7 (which used to be Dupont). You may, however, wish to use a solvent such as Prepsol or Acme's 88-Klix. These solvents will remove wax, so you should use them on the painted surfaces only if you intend to wax the car this session. You should not have to rub very hard when doing this. Let the chemicals do their job. If you are rubbing hard you are likely doing some damage to your paint. The only time you should be rubbing hard on good-condition paint is when you are polishing or buffing off the wax. The Prepsol and Klix are STRONG solvents. When applying them, do so with a rag that is dampened with the solvent rather than dripping wet with the solvent. Use sparingly so it can evaporate. If it doesn't look like it wants to evaporate, quickly wipe it off with a clean diaper.

Third, some people use baking soda to remove road tar from the painted surface. My suspicion is that the baking soda acts as a very fine-grit rubbing compound, as I do not believe that there is a chemical reaction with the tar or bugs. If my hunch is correct then you will be removing the wax and perhaps a little bit of paint as well. I think it best to avoid this.

The fourth choice is an emulsifier such as Swipe or Simple Green. This stuff is our best choice for the engine compartment and under the wheel wells and will also work on the bugs and the tar. It will, however, tend to remove the wax and so, like the solvents, should not be used on the painted surfaces unless you are going to wax the car immediately. It is a reasonable choice, if used in diluted form, to help protect the wax, but is not as effective as the solvent in removing bugs and tar. Used in too concentrated a solution these products may burn the paint.

It has also been reported that salad oil, rubbed on the tar very gently, will remove it.

Rinse, or better, rewash those areas where you have done special cleaning.

21. Dry the Car

If the day is not too windy/dusty, and the sun isn't too
bright, then you just might take the car for a very quick drive
at a brisk speed. If you do this, you will want to make the
drive very short, perhaps 1 mile or so. This will help blow
the water out of a lot of little crevices. However, if you
don't get back to your driveway and get the remaining water off
very quickly you will end up with water spots. This approach
will add a little dust to the car, but not much. It isn't
ideal, just efficient.

Do not use an air hose to dry off the car. Particles from the
air and from the air tank are projected from the nozzle at
great speed and will pit the paint.

Whether or not you drove the car to get most of the water off,
start with a diaper or terrycloth towel that has been moistened
then thoroughly wrung out. Dry cotton tends to shed water
(which is why some backpackers use cotton anoraks with
reasonable success anywhere but in Oregon; there is a limit).
The pre-moistening of the drying cloths seems more necessary
with the newer cloths. Once you have the cloths well broken in
you may be able to skip that step.

For the same reason as when washing (the bottom of the car
tends to be more dirty, even after being washed), start at the
top and work down. Also, water flows downhill, so, if you work
from the top down you won't be dripping water into your newly
dried lower parts of the car. When the rag gets soaked, wring
it out or get another. Each time you approach the car with a
fresh diaper/ towel, start as far back in your pattern as there
is any water left. That way you get to use the driest diaper
on that nearly-dry area that needs just a little bit of water
removed. Use a straight motion, not a circular one.

Be sure to dry the windows while you are drying the rest of the
car. Do not expect them to look their best just yet. The
reason that you want to dry them, even though you will clean
them later is that they will create water spots if left to dry
on their own. To some extent this is worse than water spots on
the paint, because you probably have some wax on the paint that

will make the water spots there easier to take off.   On the glass you will have no wax and so the water spots will firmly attach themselves.

If you have become used to the drying power of a chamois you are going to be disappointed with cotton.   One option that would help to quickly wring out the diapers might be to get one of those old manual wringers like you still see used at the commercial car washes.

There are also some chamois-like products on the market.   They are a brown, thin synthetic sponge of some sort, and they are stored wet, between washings, in a little plastic tube that is reasonably air tight. The one I used came well recommended. I don't think I will use it again.   It is better than a chamois in terms of being able to flush out the dirt it collects, but I don't think it is better enough.

If you just can't abide not using the chamois (and, while I disagree with your conclusion I am sympathetic to your objectives), then you need to follow a very careful procedure. First, wash VERY CAREFULLY. Second, NEVER use the chamois around the bumpers or on the lower parts of the car.   Third, clean the chamois as thoroughly as you can when you are finished drying the car. You might be able to keep it clean enough to avoid the worst of the paint scratches. If you want some moral support in this you might note that Malm's, who make well-respected waxes and ultra-fine polishes, also advocate and sell chamoix.   Jay Kolinsky, President of Malm's, seriously disputes the notion that the chamois pulls wax off the car, though he did not argue that the chamois has some tendency to retain any dirt that it picks up. I have concluded that using a chamois to dry a car is simply not the best choice.

In addition to drying the car after washing it, you might consider drying the car when putting it in the garage after you have been driving it in the rain. This is not crazy if you are normally keeping your car super-spiffy and it only takes three or four minutes, even if you do a careful job. The rain water, along with the dust in the air, will cause water spots if not properly dried.   Hose off the lower parts of the car to remove the loose mud before drying-after-rainy-driving.

22. Cleaning the Glass

Glass is very easy to clean, and there are several ways to go
about it.   You can use a little ammonia in water and you can
add a little white vinegar.   Ammonia is the key ingredient as
it does an excellent job of cutting through any film of grease
on the glass and tends to leave no residue.   Sudsy ammonia is
the best choice.   It cleans better than standard ammonia.   It
will have a very small tendency to leave more of a residue, but
you will never notice it.   The old standby, Windex, also works
well for cleaning glass.

This water/ammonia/vinegar solution will also tend to cut wax,
however, and you must be sure that your cleaning solution does
not get onto the painted surfaces (or into the leather when you
are cleaning the inside of the windows).   There is also a
product called Glass Wax.   It apparently is trying to wax and
protect the glass as well as clean it.   While the windows look
great when you are done, the process is more difficult than
water/ammonia /vinegar and will leave a dusty residue all over
the freshly washed and/or waxed car.   There are also consistent
reports that the use of Glass Wax will lead to a rainbowing
effect on the glass, as if the glass had a light coat of oil.
I don't think the trouble is worth it.

After swabbing on your chosen window-cleaning solution, wipe
off with a clean, dry cloth.   For the glass, which is much more
difficult to scratch than paint, you can use old t-shirts or
paper towels.   Both of these will have less tendency than the
diapers to shed lint.   If the diapers work for you then use
them.   You will normally need two diapers, one to get most of
the water and one to get the last of the water and bring the
glass to a high luster.   In addition to cleaning both sides of
the windows,   don't forget the interior and exterior mirrors
when cleaning the glass.   The mirrors will need adjusting when
you are through with this.

Some cars have rear-window defoggers that are glued onto the
inside surface of the glass, rather than being imbedded in the
glass.   In such cases you must be extra careful when cleaning
the rear window.   Swab and dry along the run of the wires, not
across them.

23. Removing Decals

Decals and stickers that have been applied to the glass (someone has been time trialing!?) can pose serious opportunities. The first thing to try is your window cleaning solution. Be patient: soak the decal as well as you can. If this doesn't work you can get more aggressive. Since glass is very hard to damage with chemicals I usually pull off as much of the sticker as I can, then use a cloth dampened in lacquer thinner to remove the glue and remaining parts of the sticker. Razor blades work, but you must be careful as razors will scratch glass. This means that you cannot use razor blades on the inside curve of glass, since each end of the razor will be creating a scratch mark. On flat surfaces or outside curves the razor is a real help with the thick stickers that are difficult to completely soak through with the lacquer thinner. DO NOT DRIP THE LACQUER THINNER ON ANYTHING, paint or leather, inside the car or outside.

Another approach with decals is a heat gun or hair dryer. Most glues will soften with heat, and you can lift the decal right off (use a rag so you don't toast your pinkies!). Be aware, however, than you should not get any glass or painted surface excessively hot. In the case of the glass you will risk drying out and/or cooking the nearby rubber window seals and any body or interior parts in the neighborhood. If the decal is on paint (which is absurd, but it happens) you can probably get it off. Try using Prepsol or Acme 99-Klix before you reach for the heat gun or hair dryer. Do not use lacquer thinner to remove decals from paint unless you are also going to paint the car this cleaning session. The heated decal should yield before the paint is too hot, but be very careful.

While we are on the topic of decals, it should be mentioned that you should never ever ever use masking tape on your car for any purpose other than separating areas that are to be painted from areas that are not to be painted. Most tapes that look yellow have a very high acid content in the glue. This is similar to the acid in newsprint causing newspapers to turn yellow over time, especially if left in the sun.

Masking tape is among the highest in acid content.   This will
etch and burn the paint.   It almost seems, given enough time,
that the masking tape etches the paint.   This is unlikely,
since the acids in the adhesive resin are hydorchloric and
sulfuric acids, not hydrofluoric acid. Masking tape that has
been well baked-on in the sun will come off only with razor
blades.

24. Plastic and Plexiglas

The rear windows of convertibles (and any cars with plexiglas
rear windows) need very special treatment.   Both the plastic
and the plexiglas are very subject to scratching.   When
washing, be sure to flood with water and wash very gently.
Meguiar's Mirror Glaze Professional Plastic Cleaner can be used
to polish and remove surface scratches.   This should be
followed by an application of Meguiar's Mirror   Glaze
Professional Plastic Polish.   I have also heard very good
reports about Eagle1 Plastic Polish for dealing with light
scratches.   Heavily scratched material will need the Meguiar's
two-step process.

These same products can be used to freshen up exterior plastic
such as taillight lenses that have surface scratches or a dull
appearance.

25. Cleaning the Rubber

There are several options for cleaning rubber. All of them are
essentially designed to protect the rubber.   We will cover
these issues under protecting the exterior in section 39.

26. Water Spots

One thing you will not easily see when washing the car is water
spots from being parked in the rain,   parked too near a
garden/lawn sprinkler or from previous sloppy washing.   These
spots really only show up when a car is dry, unless they are
quite severe or you have developed an exceptionally keen eye

for them. A dirty car that is lightly rained on will look a little spotty, but this is often just a reorganization of the uniform layer of dirt on the car. Most of this type of dirt should come off easily with a normal washing. However, water, especially tap water, and very especially softened water, when left to dry on the car's surface, will leave the residues of salts and calcium that are dissolved in the water. Often these spots will show up on the wheel rim, right where the bottom of the rim was when the water evaporated.

You would think that, if these salts were originally dissolved in the water they would happily dissolve right back into the water you are using to wash the car. This is, unfortunately, not at all the case. The most effective approach seems to be normal household vinegar, which is a mild acid. Use it mixed half and half with water, to see if that will get the job done. If not, use it full strength. Do not rub too hard, let the vinegar do the work. Once the spots are off, rinse the area very well. I am not sure whether the vinegar takes of the wax, but I always rewax the area just in case. Vinegar will attack aluminum and gold-like trim, so do not get any of your vinegar solution on these parts. Water spots on polished (and un-anodized) aluminum will come off with Simichrome.

Soft water helps soap and detergent to be more effective, but is not necessarily any particular help for car cleaning or water spotting. Household water softeners trade sodium for calcium (which is why you have to load them with bags and bags of salt - sodium chloride). Both will leave spots on your car. In many cases household water softeners are connected only through the household hot water supply, so you will encounter the changed chemical composition only when you are spoiling yourself and the car by washing with warm water.

Remember that, like most other contamination, water spots that have formed over a good layer of wax are much easier to remove (soap and water will usually do the trick) than if they are directly on the paint.

27. The Final Washing Step

Now that you have finished washing the car, put the various rags that you have used, along with the wash mitt (presuming that it is a cotton mitt) into the laundry to be well washed, cleansing it of oily residues and grit.

C. PROTECTING THE EXTERIOR

28. Background Information on Protecting the Exterior

The exterior should, at all times, be well protected against oxidation. This involves the use of wax or a poly sealer. Under normal use the car should be waxed every 6 months or so. Expert opinion on this varies from every three months to every twelve months. "Rejuvenating" Polyglycoat counts as waxing the car. An easy rhythm is to wax the car every other time you change the oil if your car gets a normal amount of driving. Another approach is to wax a section of the car if, while washing the car, you found a section that did not bead the water up to your satisfaction. Since a complete washing, done properly, only takes about 25 minutes on a small car, the extra 15 minutes to wax a section properly will still not make the project so long that it interferes very much with whatever else you were going to do.

In choosing the exact sequence and products for waxing a car there are three main factors at work. The first involves whether your paint is in super condition, or needs some polishing/cleaning. The second is whether you have a lacquer paint, enamel, or a newer polyurethane. The third is your personal preference about how the wax feels to use (is it easy to apply and remove) and how nice the car looks when you are done.

If your paint is in excellent condition you should not need any polish; wax only should do the job quite nicely, and with a lot less effort. Polish is not wax. Once your surface is in good shape you are looking for a wax, or a poly product, not a polish and not a cleaner.

29. Preparing Overwaxed Cars

It is possible to overwax. Most waxes will not completely
dissolve any wax already on the car, so you can add coat after
coat of wax.   The result of this will be a yellowish tone to
your paint. If you believe that you have gotten too many coats
of wax on the car you will need to use a solvent such as
Prepsol or Acme 88-Klix to strip the wax.   Be very careful
using these wax strippers.   You should use a diaper that is
moist,   but not dripping wet with the solvent.   Wipe the rag
over the surface to be stripped, then immediately follow with a
dry soft rag (diaper).   Do not let the solvent sit on the
painted surface for any length of time.   Try to do all this on
a warm day. The warmth will help whatever stripper you are not
able to wipe off to evaporate very quickly.   After doing this
stripping you should seriously consider using a pre-wax sealer
such as Meguiar's #7 Sealer and Resealer.

30. Dealing with Oxidation and Surface Scratches

If your paint is oxidized you will need to do some polishing.
Polishing is a fairly extensive topic on its own, and,   in
keeping with the objective of clarifying how to maintain a car
rather than restore it, this topic will be treated somewhat
briefly.

If your car is very badly oxidized you will need a mild rubbing
compound or heavy cleaner to get down to the good paint.
Follow this with the steps just below that are used for cars
that start out just a bit oxidized.

Some people are fond of a process called color sanding, using
very fine (1200 to 1500) wet/dry sandpaper and water.   This
process will remove paint (the harder you press the more paint
will come off), leave small scratches and require polishing as
the next step.   It is a good approach if there is plenty of
paint on the car and there is a lot of surface damage and
oxidation that has to be removed.

If your car has just a surface amount of oxidation or very fine
scratches you will need a mild polish. Meguiar's Deep Crystal

Polish and Malm's Ultra Fine Polish are good products for this. Do not use a polish, which will include some abrasives, unless you must.

You can, of course, choose one of the products that is a combined cleaner/wax. I can't prove it, but I suspect that, when you use such products, a bit of the oxidation and paint that you are removing ends up imbedded in the wax on your car. I also think that the wax must make it more difficult to achieve the polishing/abrasive action that gets all the stuff off the surface of the car in the first place. By regular care you will not need a polishing agent. If you do, I recommend that you do your polishing first, then attend to the waxing. The exception to this rule would be when waxing a car more for the purposes of protecting the car than for making it look its very best. I use a one-step cleaner/wax on a large camper van; my objectives are to prevent paint oxidation and leave the van looking basically presentable. I don't think it would be worth it to do two separate passes on such a large vehicle.

A second option, for mild oxidation, or as a step following the use of rubbing compound or color sanding on more seriously oxidized cars, is machine buffing. A finishing compound such as Liquid Ebony, when used with a buffer, gives the car an incredibly nice surface. Practice this on SOME CAR YOU DON'T CARE VERY MUCH ABOUT, as it it easy to burn the paint when first using a buffer. If you rent or buy a buffer, be sure to get the 'lay-down' type, with the polishing head at right angles to the motor. The simpler approach of using a buffer attachment on your drill gives you a tool that has too high a center of gravity and is much too unstable, and your risks of burning the paint are much too great. I am not saying that polishing cannot be done with a drill, only that, by the time you get expert enough to do this you will not like how your car already looks from the several practice sessions.

Another pre-wax treatment that is said to offer excellent results involves filling in the scratches and surface irregularities, rather than buffing them out. For this use Meguiar's #7 Sealer and Resealer. Note that it is water soluble, so once your wax is gone and you have washed the car you will have to re-apply the sealer. On the other hand, it is

pretty easy stuff with which to work. Note that it is often
much better, overall, to fill in the scratches in your car's
paint than to try to polish down below the level of the
scratches.

Keep in mind that polishing to remove scratches from the paint
(as opposed to removing a layer of oxidized paint)   requires
that you remove all the paint down to a level equal to the
bottom of the scratch.   You will achieve some results by just
removing the ridge of the scratch.   Too much of this polishing
activity and you will need more paint.

The diagrams below illustrate the various options.

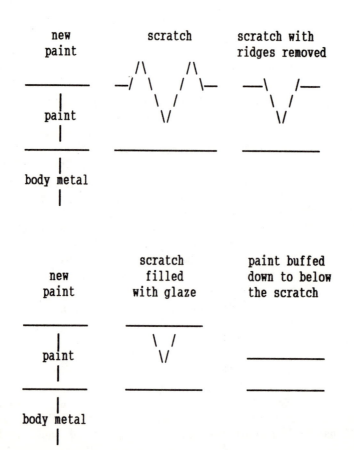

There are a few other things that we need to understand about
paint colors, paint condition, types of paints and choosing
polishes. First, dark colors will show scratches much more
than light colors. You see the scratch when light reflects off
of the ragged edges of the scratch. When you look at a white
car, there is already so much light coming off the car the
scratches are difficult to see. Not so with a dark car. The
easiest color to care for is tan (non-metallic). Scratches,
oxidation and dirt all tend to be difficult to see on tan cars.

Cars with metallic paint present special problems as they age.
They tend to deteriorate more rapidly than simple colors. This
may be due to the metallic particles bouncing the light around
inside the paint. If they are not covered with a coat of clear
paint, then you have both paint oxide and metallic oxide to
deal with as the surface deteriorates. When such paint is
allowed to become sufficiently weathered it can be very
difficult to restore.

31. Polishing and Wax Preparation Summary

Depending on the condition of your car, pick your starting
point in the list below and work your way down. When using any
polish, rub in a single direction, not in a circular motion.


```
Heavy Rubbing Compound <— paint very badly oxidized
    |                                   or scratched
    V
Heavy Cleaner or      <— paint badly oxidized or scratched
  or Mild Rubbing Compound
    V
Normal Car Polish     <— mild oxidation or mild scratches
  or Liquid Ebony
    V
Super-fine Polish     <— scratches visible only on
    |                                 careful inspection
    V
(Glaze if you like)
    V
  WAX
```

32. Choosing a Wax: Carnuba or 'Poly'

The actual process of waxing a car is fairly simple compared to
the process of choosing a wax.   The choice of which wax to use
must have gotten more serious in 1886, the year in which
Daimler and Benz built, independently, the first two cars on
the face of the earth, but I suspect the controversy has been
raging since the time of the Roman chariots or whenever people
began to add pigmentation to their vehicles.

You must consider the type of paint on the car.   If your car
has lacquer paint it wants carnuba in the wax, the more the
better. Carnuba is a natural wax, found covering the leaves of
a Brazilian Palm tree, the Coperinicia Cerifera.   The tree is
native to the rainforest, and the carnuba covers the young
leaves, helping to protect them from the sun, the heat and the
leeching effects of the heavy rain.   The demand for carnuba
would not seem to be a factor in the decimation of these
magnificent forests. After all, if you eliminate the tree you
don't get any more leaves.   Meguiar's, Harly, and Malm's and
several other manufacturers all make waxes that are primarily
carnuba.   Quist Crystal Clear has also been recommended by
people who seem to know what they are doing.   Do not use poly
products on lacquered cars.   It seems that the lacquer paint
needs to breath,   and the poly treatments seal the car too
tightly.

For cars with the newer polyurethane paint you can choose the
carnuba-intensive waxes, or you can use the poly sealers and
protectors.   The most famous of these is Polyglycoat,   but
Astroshield with dimethlpolysiloxane and polyethylene polymers
or Westley's liquid or cream with dimethlpolysiloxane are
similar products.   Another indication of a poly product is the
term   'resin   glaze'.   These poly products,   especially
Polyglycoat, are quite popular as a dealer add-on, with some
vague mumblings about permanent paint protection. However, it
seems that this permanent protection needs "renewal" on a
rather frequent basis, not less than once a year, so it is only
marginally better than the wax in terms of how long it lasts.
The main benefits of this "paint conditioning" would seem to be
to the dealer's profit margin.

[Siskin   Enterprises has taken a similar approach for
treating   leather with Perma-Plate Leatherguard and has
recently introduced Perma-Plate Fibreguard for fabrics.   See
sections 49 and 51 for more exciting details.]

Compounding   the problem of making a decision about wax is   the
conflicting   input from users of the carnuba waxes.   Some   say
that carnuba will only last for three or four washings;   others
claim that carnuba will last an entire year on a car   that   is
driven daily.

In general,   the carnuba waxes seem easier to apply and   work
with,   so,   if they lasted as long as the poly compounds   they
would,   I think, be a clear choice.   The carnubas also seem to
bead up   the   wax much better when just applied than   the   poly
compounds when they are fresh.   To a certain extent I think it
boils down to how often you are willing to wax the car, and how
much effort you are willing to put in.   If you are sure   that
the   car will only get waxed every 18   months or so,   a   poly
treatment would seem to be the best choice.   Once you get down
to waxing   every year,   or perhaps a little more   often,   the
carnuba should do the job.   One further point in favor of   the
carnuba: it seems to do a lot more good for the chrome   parts
than the poly does.

Whether you use a poly protector or carnuba,   the protector
is probably still doing some good even once water stops totally
beading up on the surface,   but the most conservative approach
is to wax often.

There is a further issue raised about the poly treatments.   It
is   said that the silicones penetrates the paint and the metal,
making repainting difficult, and causing fisheyes, for example.
According to the body shops,   the poly products will   penetrate
the paint, but not the metal.   This means that any painting you
do over a poly coating will involve either taking the   surface
down to metal,   or adding silicones to the paint.   Taking   the
car down to the metal surface is normal when repainting
valuable cars.   However, this stuff may well soak into any body
fillers that may have been used to repair the car.   If this is
true then repainting may also involve having to totally   redo
any areas where any body fillers have been used.

There is one further complication about the silicones. Evidently silicones come in active and passive forms. I have not yet gotten to the bottom of this issue.

There are many good carnuba waxes available in the marketplace. Ones with which I have had good success, or that have come highly recommended from sources I trust are Meguiar's Deep Crystal Carnuba Wax(liquid), Meguiar's Deep Crystal Carnuba Paste, Malm's Carnuba Wax, Harley Carnuba, and Quist Crystal Clear. I have tried Meguiar's Mirror Glaze Professional Paste Wax. It went on easily enough, but, unless carefully spread to a very thin layer when being applied, was somewhat difficult to wipe off. The Harly goes on very easily, but seems to leave more of a white residue when you get it on the rubber. The Malm's comes very highly recommended but is VERY expensive. I don't think you can go wrong with any of the Meguiar's products. Klasse and Classic also have their following, though some say that Klasse is more difficult to use. Klasse is a German product and is available in some stores, but seems to be sold mostly through mail order, so don't be disappointed if you don't find it on the shelf of your local auto supply store. I also would note that, compared to most American products, there is very little hard information on the label. It is very difficult to read the Klasse labels and come to any realistic conclusions about the composition of the product.

33. Waxing the Painted Surfaces

Once you have made your brand-name choice of weapons, follow the instructions for application and removal. This is important. Some waxes like to be applied with a moistened applicator, others prefer dry. Some waxes like to be wiped off nearly as soon as they are applied to the car, others will tolerate sitting for hours before they are wiped off. If you are having problems, be sure that your car is neither too cold nor too hot, that you have properly dried the car after washing, and that you are following the directions precisely. If this doesn't solve things for you, get a different wax. When you are waxing, try to keep the wax off the rubber. There are a variety of ways of getting it off later, but they are all more work than a little extra care when applying the wax.

Use diapers or 100% terrycloth towels for wax application and removal. You can also use old t-shirts for wax application if they are 100% cotton. When removing the wax the cloth will want to be turned over and/or replaced fairly frequently. If your wax will tolerate waiting around for awhile before it is wiped off, I find it very effective to wax the whole car, then go over it with one rag, getting the bulk of the wax off, but not paying a lot of attention to getting all the wax. Then get a fresh buffing rag and start at the beginning again, removing the last of the excess wax.

34. Waxing the Chrome

There is not a lot of chrome on the newer cars but the older ones have chrome bumpers and other small trim. To the extent that you find any chrome on your car it is important to care for it. Clean chrome is very easy to care for, as it loves to be waxed. Once again, the reason chrome care is important it that the surface is quite porous. Moisture penetrates through the chrome and oxidizes the metal underneath. Be sure to keep your chrome very well waxed. Also again, use Happich's Simichrome on the polished aluminum. Follow this with wax.

35. Wax Cleanup

When the waxing is done you will notice a couple of problems. There is still wax in a lot of little crevices (such as around any emblems and model designators the car is carrying), and there may be a whitish wax residue on some of the rubber.

The wax in the crevices is removed with a soft toothbrush or a soft paintbrush (2 inches wide) that has been cut off to about 3/8 inches in length. Natural bristles are preferred for all brushes that are used for caring for the car as they have tapered ends rather than the scratchy blunt cut of a nylon brush. However, natural-bristle toothbrushes are very hard to find except at your dentist. I have been pretty happy with an anti-plaque toothbrush made by Aim. In the teen size it comes in a soft version. If the brush feels gentle when used firmly on the palm of your hand it is probably OK. Be gentle when

using any brushes directly on the painted surfaces of your car.
Section 39 on rubber care will deal with removing wax residue
from the rubber.

36. Waxing the Wheels

Wheels need protection. This need is particularly great on all
cars with disk brakes. The brake pad dust that tends to coat
the wheels is very acidic and will tend to eat through the
wheel as well as any clear anodization and/or paint on the
wheels. It's pretty hard on chrome wheels as well. All this
can ruin (for aesthetic purposes) four very expensive pieces of
your car. The best option for keeping the wheels protected is,
each time you wash the car, to spray the wheels well with
Pledge household furniture wax and wipe it off. If you have
the patience very frequently to use a regular car wax on the
wheels, so much the better. Frequent use of Pledge will do the
job.   In any case, you should wipe the brake dust off of the
wheels as often as possible. Every time you drive the car
would not be too often.

According to the new Porsche owner's manual, the alloy wheels
should be protected with a thin coat of Vaseline. This would
work for any alloy wheel. I believe that the Vaseline serves
its protective function fairly well, but not without some
drawbacks. While it is providing a protective layer which the
brake dust can hardly penetrate, the Vaseline is quite sticky
and it tends to collect every piece of brake dust, road grit,
bird and small pet that comes anywhere near the wheel surface.
For good appearance you will need to wipe the wheels off and
re-apply the Vaseline very frequently. This might be the best
choice for those who must drive cars with alloy wheels on snowy
and salted roads. Simply put a thickish coat of vaseline on
the wheels and leave it there for the winter.

37. Protection in the Engine Compartment and Trunk

The engine compartment and under the hood are not supposed to
look like the main painted surfaces of the exterior, but they
do need some protection in order to stay new-like. Fortunately

this protection is very easy to provide.   Under the hood/trunk
and inside the engine cover use Lemon Pledge spray wax.   Spray
it on and wipe it off.   On the rest of the engine and engine
compartment you have a couple of choices.   One is the Pledge,
and,   except where it will get pretty hot and burn off,   it
should provide adequate protection. You can also spray a light
oil.   WD-40   contains a light oil and some very volatile
solvents that aid it in its job a penetrating agent, loosening
corroded nuts and bolts and the like.   These solvents will
evaporate rather rapidly, leaving a fine coating of oil that
will protect most surfaces.   This has to be done fairly often
for the best effect, but it is easy to do and is the treatment
that I prefer.   Whichever you choose,   spray it on the engine
compartment sheet metal,   and on any parts that don't get
especially hot.   There are some hardcore car lovers and
concours fanatics who like to keep their engine washed.   I
think this is far too difficult on most of the modern cars in
which the the engine compartment tends to be chock full of all
manner of mechanical and electronic wizardry.   In any case, oil
is not needed if you keep the engine washed,   but you might try
Simichrome on the aluminum parts.

38. Undercoating

It is very easy,   during this part of car care,   to look at the
undercoating, at least that part that you can easily see in the
wheel wells and such,   and see if some of it has gotten knocked
loose.   If so,   given that you have done a good job of washing
and rinsing, and everything has had a good chance to dry, you
can spray on some undercoating and get back most of the
protection you had when the car left the factory.   If the car
is routinely exposed to salted roads this will not be a
complete solution,   but it will help.   The rust process that
begins when salt and moisture are trapped in the car will not
be deterred quite so simply.   However, if the problem is merely
that the undercoating has been mechanically knocked around,
then spraying on some more is a very easy form of additional
protection.

39. Rubber-Care Products

If you crave adventure, jumping out of airplanes, flying
gliders or ultra-lights, Golden Gate Region time trials or
having affairs with the wives of police chiefs, you might want
to go to the next concours and shout out "Get your nice fresh
Armor All here!" It will give rubber (and vinyl) a new-like
appearance, though a bit wet-looking, what the concours people
call 'over-prepared'. However, once you start this, it seems
you have to keep it up on a routine basis. According to the
stories I have heard, if you stop applying the product, the
rubber will rather quickly turn brown and look terrible. The
rubber has essentially developed a drug-like dependency on the
Armor All.

There is a problem standing in the way of pulling this issue
properly apart: the common complaint about Armor All is that
the rubber will develop a dependency on the product. Yet this
information is typically coming from concours-oriented people
who will be religiously using Clean Eze or a Meguiar's product
on a very frequent basis. Unless they intentionally let their
car deteriorate a bit I can't see whether they could ever find
out if the rubber develops a similar dependency on the products
they are using.

It is normally said that the problem with Armor All is the
silicones it contains. The theory is that silicones lead to
deterioration of rubber. Interestingly, essentially all
products on the market that are designed for treating rubber
contain silicones. This includes those products advocated by
the same concours people who so intensely dislike Armor All.

There are three rubber-care products that seem to have better
reputations. First, there is Clean Eze. It smells like
kerosene. Many people have reported very good success with
this product. Clean Eze contains some silicones. There are
aesthetic reasons (smell) for not using it in the interior of
the car. The other two products are from Meguiar's. Formula
40 is a water-based product and can be used on rubber and
vinyl. Formula 42 is petroleum-based and is designed for the
newer-style rubber bumpers. The Meguiar's representative
suggested that Formula 42 would sometimes setup with a whitish

film on tires.   This is similar to a comment made that rubber on which Armor All had been used would turn white if subject to temperatures over 140 degrees Fahrenheit. Tires can easily get this hot.   After extended discussions with product support people at Meguiar's I found that Formulas 40 & 42 also contain silicones.   There are other products available, but none seem, to me, to have any merits over these three.

Obviously it is not possible to determine exactly how much silicone is in each of these products, as the formulas are carefully protected.   It may be that a little silicone is a good thing, but too much is bad.   Nor have I found anyone who can explain why the rubber people are so opposed to silicones, yet one finds silicones in essentially all the rubber-care products.   Clearly someone thinks the silicones, at least in some amount, are necessary.

You may also wish to look into what seems to be a new class of products on the market.   One of these,   from Ameritech Industries, is 303 Protectant.   The product claims that it has no silicones or petroleum distillates, will not remove wax, and blocks ultraviolet rays.   I am not sure what to make of all this,   but I think I will experiment a little bit on my non-Porsche first.

My recommendation is to either use Clean Eze on all external rubber, and Meguiar's Formula 40 on the rubber inside the car, or use Meguiar's Formula 42 on the bumpers and external trim, and Meguiar's formula 40 everywhere else.

Normally you will want to let the product sit on and soak into the rubber for awhile, then wipe it off.   Include the spoiler lip, bumpers, mirror guards, trunk trim.   Application can be from a spray bottle for big areas, q-tips for very tight crevices, or, for those nasty pleats on the ends of the newer bumpers,   a 1-inch-wide paint brush that has been cut down to about 1 inch in length.   You can rough up the ends of this brush by rubbing on concrete until you have a very soft swab.

The removal of any wax on the rubber can be done with the toothbrush and some Clean Eze.   The easiest thing is to keep the wax off the rubber. This is especially important on the rough-surface rubber used on the newer models and/or rubber than has not been protected with Meguiar's or Clean Eze.

There is another product for rubber, a very old-fashioned one called Rubber-Lube. It used to be very popular at Standard stations. I did not find it at any retail outlet and have no idea what is in it. I have to suspect that it is loaded with silicones. I also seem to remember, from my days as a Chevron pump jockey, that the stuff had an impressive bouquet.

An additional option for tires is to paint them with tire paint. This will give them a very black look, something a little too shiny to look just like new. However, after a couple of weeks the tires settle down to looking very nice. Some of these tire painting products are a bit thick. They can be thinned with paint thinner (acrylic enamel thinner was suggested) if they are petroleum-based, or with water if water-based. Thin only what you are using, not the whole can.

If you are using tires with very soft compounds, trying to get that last extra bit of cornering power, you may find that you wear the tires out pretty quickly. In this case you can safely use whatever you wish on the tires.

40. Car Covers

Car covers, properly used, are one of the best ways to protect your car, inside and out. The car will get dirty more slowly and it will be protected, when covered, from much of the harmful effects of the sun. Though some of the dust does come through, it is almost like having the car in the garage all the time. The sun protection is especially important for leather interiors. It is relatively quick to put a cover over a car as small as a Porsche or to remove the cover. The typical time for me, without help, is 18 seconds. A little longer in high winds, if I am carrying something in one hand or if I have assistance. I also use a cover for the camper van since the van is too tall to fit into the garage. While it is a bit of a chore to get the cover on and off, the van looks better after three months under the cover than after one week sitting out without the cover.

Car covers are especially helpful for convertible owners,
particularly those people who prefer to drive with the top down
most of the time.   One of the hassles of a convertible is
having to choose, every time you stop the car, between leaving
the car open to the sun, wind, dust and strangers, or going
through the effort of putting the top up. A car cover protects
the car from the sun and most of the dust.   It also seems to
have an impact on vehicle security.   In areas where there are
lots of people around, such as at shopping centers or corporate
parking   lots,   most people will not take the public risk of
lifting a cover to see what is underneath.   If you have an
uncovered car people with evil intentions can, just by looking
through   the   window,   check out the stereo system and any
belongings you have left in the car.   With a covered car they
have to touch it before they even know it's worth the risk.
While granting that using a car cover as a security measure
will not be sufficient in the Bronx or other high-crime areas,
it nevertheless seems to provide a real deterrent to people
messing with the car in some situations.

One last commercial for car covers, then we can proceed.   When
the evily careless person parked next to you bangs his/her door
open against your car, the cover will provide a little bit of
chip and scratch protection.   Until such people are forced to
strap inner tubes to all doors we need all the protection we
can get.

If you get a cover, get one that is 100% cotton.   Synthetic
covers are   rougher on the paint as they flap in the breeze.
Some of them will even trap water under the cover, leading to
mildew and other problems.   I get mine from Beverly Hills
Motoring Accessories.   I think there are good covers available
for less money, but I have always been pleased with the product
and the service.

There are some cautions about using a car cover.   You should
not cover a car that is very dirty. The cover will move around
a little as you put it on the car, and it will flap a little
bit if there is any wind.   This movement will tend to use the
grit on the car to sand the paint.   Note, however, that the
proper way of installing the cover is NOT to drag it over the
surface.   Rather, you should have folded the cover up as a part

of the process of taking it off the car the last time you used it. To put the cover on the car, unfold in the exact reverse sequence. This will help to minimize any scratching from the car cover. If you regularly use a car cover the car will stay much cleaner than you would expect. My approach is to cover the car at essentially all times, and wash it every week or two. During this time, under normal conditions, you should not pick up enough dirt on the car to be dangerous. Do NOT start using a cover after the car has been sitting out without a cover unless you wash the car.

Wash the car cover every month or so. Remember, it is collecting all the dirt that would otherwise be getting on the car. You want to get rid of that dirt.

Car covers wear out. If your cover sits most days in the sunlight, protecting your car from the sun and the dirt you can be sure that the cotton will wear out. First it will soften and fade. The softness will actually make it better on the paint, and the fade will suggest to would-be car molesters that nothing of great value lies underneath. Later the cover will begin to tear very easily if you catch it on something sharp. At about your third trip to the sewing machine to fix a few small rips you should call up your favorite car cover supplier and order a new one. Figure that the car cover, which sells for about $110 will last about 2-3 years. Cheap compared to $3,000 or so to properly repaint the car whose paint will eventually fade if the car is routinely left in the sun. Your interior, kept cooler and out of the worst of the suns rays will also be in much better shape for your efforts.

41. Bras

Bras are OK when the car is in motion, but left out in the sun their black color causes them to get VERY HOT. Under these circumstances they can cause serious heat damage to your paint job. They also tend to trap moisture from rain, or fog between themselves and the paint. This, too, can lead to paint damage. The best use for a bra is to install it before you will be driving the car through airborne debris (dirt roads, time trials where some cars have race tires that are sticky enough

to pick the grit off the track and throw it at your car, long
trips across the country) and then remove the cover when you
park the car. Obviously you want to find a bra that is very
easy to install and remove. If you use a car cover at all
times when the car is stopped, then you can leave the bra on
except when things get damp out.

42. Minor Paint Touchup

With continued driving the paint on the car will get chipped
from small rocks thrown up into the air by the tires of cars
ahead of you or cars going the other direction on narrow roads.
While it is a bit of a tedious process, a little bit of work
touching up the paint can keep the car much better looking
until such time as the car, or a portion of it, has to be
repainted for other reasons.

The touchup process works quite well for one-stage, non-
metallic paints. It works marginally for two-stage, metallic
paints. It is still worth doing on a metallic paint job, as it
is a very bad idea to leave the underlying sheet metal exposed
to the air, but owners of cars with metallic paint jobs need to
have very limited expectations about how invisible the repair
will end up being.

Touch up should be done right after waxing. This will allow
the paint you apply to dry and cure in the three to nine months
before you wax the car again.

Use Prepsol along with q-tips to clean off the wax in and
around all the paint chips you are going to touch up. Be sure
to wipe off the Prepsol quickly.

Locate the proper paint to touch up your car. Car dealers
sometimes carry a touch up pencil, which is just that. Do not
use this. The dealers should also carry, at least for the
newer colors, proper touch up paint. If you cannot find the
paint you need at the dealer, most color shops (stores that
provide for the needs of the body shops) will mix the color you
need from the formula or custom match the exact current color
of your car. The custom-match approach is the best. The

charge for this, at least in Northern California, is about $15 over the cost of the paint itself. Good body shops will also custom-match paint, but their charges for the labor to do the color match tend to be higher.

One-stage paint (no clear overcoat): using a very small brush, apply a thin layer of paint into the chip area. If the paint on the car is thick, you will need to let the first coat dry, then come back with another thin layer. Continue this until the touchup paint is higher, by just a little bit, than the surrounding paint.

Two-stage paint (color first layer with a clear overcoat): using a very small brush, apply a thin layer of the colored paint into the bottom of the chip area. Let this dry. Return later to overpaint with the clear overcoat. Do this in stages, a thin layer of overcoat each time until the clear coat is just a little bit higher than the surrounding paint. Let the paint dry for at least 12 hours between coats.

Once the touchup paint is fully dry (allow about a week) you can rub it down to the level of the surrounding paint. Start by masking off the area around the chip with masking tape. This will help prevent your efforts in improving the car from causing any additional damage to the surrounding areas. Use #600 wet/dry sandpaper, well wetted, to sand the chip nearly down to the level of the surrounding paint. Next, use 1200 or 1500 wet/dry sandpaper, well wetted to get the surface smoother and down a little lower. At this point you have to take off the masking tape. Next use a very mild rubbing compound to bring the surface to a higher luster. Finally, use a polishing compound such as Meguiar's Deep Crystal Polish (or a buffer and some Liquid Ebony) to bring the paint to a luster. You must leave the touchup spot unwaxed until the next time you wax the car so the touch up paint can have a chance to cure. The curing process is mostly one of allowing ALL the solvents in the paint to completely evaporate.

D. CLEANING THE INTERIOR

While it is quite nice to have the outside of the car protected and looking gorgeous, it is the inside of the car where you spend most of your car time. Care here is important both to keep the car in good shape and to get the most enjoyment out of the car.

43. Vacuum the Inside of the Car

Vacuuming is one of the most important things you can do for the interior of the car. The carpets are especially in need of frequent vacuuming. Dirt works its way down into the carpet where its sharp edges cut the carpet fibers every time you step on the carpet. You need to vacuum much more often than you need to do the rest of the interior cleaning. We are covering this activity at this point in the series as it is a logical part of cleaning the interior. However, on a normal washday for your car you might want to vacuum first, so that whatever water you track into the car while washing it does not turn into mud quite so easily.

The best vacuum is a reasonably strong wet/dry shop vacuum, though you can achieve perfectly acceptable results with a household canister vacuum. Try to leave the vacuum near where you park the car and plugged into the wall. Since you want to vacuum often you want to make it very easy for yourself to do this job. Use a crevice tool on the end. The crevice tool looks like it won't cover much territory, but you are going after some fairly reluctant dirt and you want to be properly armed. You will actually get the car cleaner with this tool, and it really doesn't take any longer. Remove everything that is going to be in your way. Leave the floor mats in to start. Vacuum everything. Don't forget in the storage areas, armrest hidey-holes, down in any folds of the seat upholstery, the trunk, etc. After the removable floor mats are vacuumed remove them from the car and keep vacuuming. This will take a little bit of time, but it is rewarding work, as you can see things getting cleaner as you move along.

The other interior cleaning does not need to be done nearly so
often as the vacuuming.   Depending on how severe (and dusty)
your environment is,   every three months or so should be
sufficient.

44.   Cleaning the Floormats and Other Carpeting

Mix up some carpet shampoo or a mild solution of Woolite in
water.   Working on a flat surface, hose down the floor mats
with water.   Use the Woolite solution to scrub down the floor
mats.   Don't be afraid to work up lots of suds.   When they are
clean, rinse thoroughly.   These will take a couple of days to
dry, and will dry most effectively if hung vertically.   If the
carpets have rubber parts sewn onto them, hang the carpets with
the rubber end up.

Use the Woolite or shampoo solution to scrub the dirty spots of
the carpeting that cannot be easily removed.   Do not over-soap
these areas.   The problem with these carpet areas is that we
cannot completely flush with water; the soap solution will have
to be gotten out with the wet/dry shop vacuum.   So, in these
cases, we want to be a little more careful about how much soap
we use.

There are also spray carpet cleaners.   Turtlewax Carpet Cleaner
and Protector is commonly available and simple to use: spray it
on, rub it in, let it dry (two to four hours) and vacuum it
away.

Any areas that still seem dirty can be attacked with a super-
emulsifier like Swipe.   Use a very mild solution (50:1).   Once
you have applied the Swipe and scrubbed, vacuum the area.   Then
scrub with a brush rinsed in clear water and vacuum.   Repeat
this water/vacuum process two or three times, until it is
reasonable to believe that the Swipe is mostly gone.   There are
also spray cans to help with spotting.   Scotchguard and
Turtlewax both market spray spot removers.

You may occasionally (and sadly) find that you have tracked inside your car some of the chewing gum that some thoughtless people throw onto the ground in parking lots. Fortunately this almost always ends up on the removable floor mats rather than on the leather or other areas that are more difficult to clean. Most carpets will stand up quite nicely to some very serious cleaning efforts. Pick out by hand all of the chewing gum that you can. Then wash the carpets per the instructions above. Great diligence in the washing may get all of the gum out. If the gum is still in the carpet you will have to resort to more aggressive measures. I haven't tried it, but I think a hair dryer or heat gun might get the gum soft enough that you could blot it away with an absorbent rag. If all of this fails, then pour lacquer thinner onto the gum spot and scrub with a stiff natural-bristle brush. With a little patience and a little more lacquer thinner the gum will dissolve. Flush with a little more lacquer thinner to get all the dissolved gum out of the carpet, (if you don't do this the dissolved gum will remain after the lacquer thinner is gone, setting up the carpet as generally stiff and gummy) and then completely rewash the area with soap and water. Do not imagine that this process is without its own risks. The lacquer thinner is very strong material and may affect some dyes. It will also be fairly hard on any rubber or vinyl trim on the floormat. If there are moisture barriers built into the carpet they will probably be dissolved by the lacquer thinner. Be careful, and test first if you are at all concerned that you may damage something.

45. Cleaning the Non-leather Parts of the Interior

Wipe all non-leather parts of the interior with a damp diaper. Includes guages, vents, steering wheel, etc. Use q-tips to get into the tight spots. Note that you should keep in your cleaning kit only the wood-stem q-tips. You will have occasion to use q-tips with heavier solvents which will melt the plastic stems used on the cheaper q-tips, leaving a real mess. If there is a grease film or a film from smoking cigarettes (or worse), dip the diaper in a mild (diluted) ammonia solution, wring it out and proceed. The ammonia will cut the film very easily. Keep a cloth that has been treated with ammonia away from the leather. If the interior is fairly clean you can skip

this step and just wipe down the interior non-leather parts
with Lemon Pledge wax. The insides of well used ashtrays can
be cleaned by soaking in Swipe. Rinse and dry

46. Cleaning the Vinyl

In addition to the water wipedown, vinyl can be cleaned with
any of the vinyl/rubber/leather products. Meguiar's Formula 40
would be a reasonable choice. I use a 10:1 dilution of Swipe
first, then follow with the Formula 40, which has some ability
to protect the vinyl.

47. Cleaning the Leather

Wipe leather with damp cloth, then use a dry diaper to wipe
dry. Be sure to get down inside the various crevices of the
seat when doing this. You will be amazed at the amount of dirt
piled up in the crevices. If the leather does not come clean
with a simple wipedown, use Lexol's leather cleaner to get it
nice and spiffy. This must be followed with a leather
restorative and preserver. Leather care will be covered more
fully later in section 49.

48. Special Interior Cleaning Issues

If your seats are fabric, shampoo them as you would the carpet
and vacuum them very dry. They will retain moisture for
awhile, so the car will need to sit while they dry out (or you
will need a rain slicker to drive!).

You will not find lacquer thinner on the parts list, but, in
all fairness, it should be mentioned that lacquer thinner will
cut almost anything, including the paint on your car and vinyl
and plastic in your interior. The proper uses for this are in
getting paint off of things, like carpet, that can stand up the
the lacquer thinner. One source noted that it will also take
shoe marks off the vinyl. To be used in this way it must be
applied with a rag that is moist but not soaked, and you have
to be pretty quick. If you really rub it into the vinyl the

vinyl will turn sticky, melt and dissolve.   Another super-
dissolver is Valspar Vinyl Paint Reducer.   Vinyl paint is used
on the bottoms of boats, and this is the reducer or thinner for
that paint.   Be very careful with all this.   Do not get any of
this stuff on any interior plastic.   Also note that these
products are very hard on your skin, bad for your lungs and
quite flammable.

E. PROTECTING THE INTERIOR

49. Protecting Leather Upholstery

Excepting perhaps the choice of wax for the painted surfaces or
choosing a product for rubber care, there does not seem to be
any area that inspires quite so much controversy as the care of
leather. Leather does get dirty, yet great care must be
taken in the cleaning of it. First, some background.

Essentially all automotive leather is surface-dyed rather than
vat dyed. Actually, what we might imagine vat-dyeing to be is
not a process that is used by the leather industry. Leather is
dyed either by what is essentially a spray painting process,
applied to only the conditioned and buffed side, or the hides
are run through rollers while aniline (alcohol-solution) dyes
are poured on both sides. There is a very limited range of
colors available in aniline dyes. Since the interior designers
want to have reasonable freedom in designing color
combinations, it is the spray-dyed leather that ends up in our
cars. Note that some manufacturers, Porsche included, still
offers leather interiors on a match-to-customer-provided-sample
basis, totally ruling out the use of aniline dyes.

It has been reported that modern American automotive leather is
often coated with some sort of a vinyl, resin or plastic
coating, helping it to resist staining and absorbing moisture.
It is certain that the modern American automotive leather is
treated in some ways to help make it resistant to water and
alcohol. The extent to which this will also reduce the ability
of the leather to breath is not clear. It is this breathing
ability, not the status appeal, that is the great asset of
leather upholstery. Because the leather can breath it is more
comfortable on a hot day, whereas vinyl will trap moisture in
your clothes. Perforating the vinyl is a help, but still not
as good as leather.

The coating on the leather may cause the leather treatment
products not to be absorbed. You will need to experiment a

bit.   If you can't tell the difference between areas you treat
and   areas you do not treat,   and if it seems that nothing is
soaking in,   then you will have to treat the leather more or
less like vinyl.   In no case should you use heavy cleaners on
any type of leather.

Siskin Enterprises appears to have taken a lesson from the book
of Polyglycoat and provides a dealer-applied treatment for
leather & vinyl. Their trade name is Perma-Plate Leatherguard.
It is designed to protect leather and vinyl.   For three years
after dealer application the leather or vinyl is guaranteed not
to fade or deteriorate.   "Any damaged area will be   replaced
completely free of charge," says the leaflet.   As one would
expect, the Warranty Protection System (their term, not mine)
comes with a "Renewer bottle".   My own view on this is that
good leather is likely to last three years with very little
maintenance.   Further, if this stuff seals up the leather (on
leather that has not already been sealed by the leather
processor), then you have lost the breathability that is one of
the real advantages of leather.   If your leather is already
sealed up then you ought to treat it much like vinyl,   and I
have a difficult time believing that any sealer like this will
help much.

Hide Food is a one-step process, and will add the required oils
to the leather.   It will not clean the leather very well. Use
Hide Food if your leather came clean with a water wipe-down and
just needs some oil and moisture replenishment. This should be
done frequently.

Lexol has two leather-care products on the market: a   leather
cleaner and an oil. Use of the oil without the cleaner is said
to lead to a build-up of surface film, and a hard leather
surface, though others have disputed this.   The Lexol cleaner
is some kind of a soap, at least it acts like a diluted soap.
Use the cleaner if you need more than water to get the leather
clean.   You can follow up with Lexol or Hide Food.   I   still
prefer the Hide Food, as it seems to penetrate directly into
the leather and leave no oily film on the surface but long-term
use by other people indicates that the Lexol is just fine.

If you really feel that your leather needs some serious
rejuvenation you can use Rejuvenator Oil from Leatherique
Restoration Products. This company, in Florida, has done a lot
of work figuring out what oils are in the leather to start
with; the product puts back into the leather exactly what has
been oxidizing and evaporating away. The product is 90% animal
oils, compared to an estimated 10% in Lexol and Hide Food. It
is worth a small order to these people just for the literature
they send along about leather and its care and restoration.
They recommend that Rejuvenator Oil be applied to leather once
a year, but I think I will just continue on with Hide Food
until it become apparent that something else is needed.

Mink Oil has been said by several people to discolor the
leather and the clothing of the people who sit on the leather.
Since the leather is surface-dyed, the discoloration may not be
apparent on the surface but is probably going on underneath the
color you see. This seems like unnecessary risks as long as
Hide Food does the job and you use it often enough. Neats Foot
Oil, popular among the horsey crowd for care of saddles and the
like, would seem to operate like the Mink Oil.

The use of Saddle Soap should be reserved for leather that is
downright filthy and did not clean up with Lexol Leather
Cleaner. Saddle soap is said to clog the pores of the leather,
leading to a solid-looking, worn-leather look.

50. Renewing Interior Rubber

The procedures for the interior rubber are basically the same
as for the exterior and were covered in section 39. Use
Meguiar's Formula 40 for the interior rubber.

51. Treatment of the Rest of the Interior

The parts of the interior that are not leather, rubber, vinyl,
fabric or carpet should be wiped down with a diaper onto which
you have sprayed Lemon Pledge. Turn the cloth frequently. If
you are fond of Scotchguard you might want to carefully spray
some on the carpeted sections of your car and on the seats if

they are fabric.   This is especially recommended if you
transport children,   especially if such children bring icecream
or   sodas   into the car.   You may also wish to consider Siskin
Enterprises' Perma-Plate Fibreguard, sometimes available at the
dealer   when   you buy a new car.   They   guarantee   to   protect
fabric interiors against staining for five years.   Seems to me
that the Scotchguard should do,   but I   could be   wrong.   Use
Q-tips to clean the tightly contoured areas, such as around the
radio and in the airconditioner vent grills.

52. Dealing with Smells

As   a final touch you may want to spray the carpet in   the   car
with Lysol once you have completed the cleaning process.   This
leaves   the   car smelling a bit fresher for a couple   of   days.
You   can   also get cans of new-car odor,   though it   should   be
mentioned   that   they will make your car smell more like a   new
Ford than a new Porsche.

F. FINAL THOUGHTS

53. Finding a Detailer

Having read this far you may nevertheless contemplate the work involved in keeping your car clean and protected and find that you really wish to spend your time in other ways. This is no great crime. Nor does it mean that your car has to suffer, which is a good thing, because, ultimately, if your car suffers you will in some ways also suffer. Your best approach is to locate two or three detailers that you might consider using. Before you even take the time to sit and talk with them they should have come well-recommended by someone whose judgement in such matters you trust. As a last resort you can go through the yellow pages, but that means that you'd better have more candidates, probably six or so.

The product that a detailer produces should be both a car that is extremely clean and shiny right now, as well as a car that is properly protected from the environment for a few months. Unfortunately it is a lot easier to evaluate how clean the car is now than it is to evaluate how well the car is protected. Some detailers concentrate mostly on the 'right now' aspects, and this is a shame, because the protection, once the car is clean, is relatively easy to provide. Others detailers, well meaning though they may be, are simply not sufficiently informed about the products that they are using and end up using products that are, to one degree or another, harmful to the car. All detailers are subject to the temptation to reach for a stronger chemical than is needed, just because they can be relatively sure that the chemical will work. Not all detailers yield to such temptations. For all these reasons it is critical that you find out exactly what the detailer plans to do to your car.

Some detailers are most reluctant to talk about such things. They seem to have a belief that their secret of success is in the chemical products, rather than in their diligence, experience and sweat. This is unfortunate. However, I will

not let anyone work on my car unless I know exactly what they
plan to do.   I'm sure that I have avoided using some people
that are quite good, but I still have my peace of mind.

You may also wish to consider whether you prefer a detailer who
works alone,   or a shop with several employees.   I tend to
prefer the person working alone, but I'm not sure it is a
rational prejudice.

With each person, meet them wherever is convenient.   Ask them
to review for you their entire cleaning and protection process.
Be sure that they understand that you want to know the
chemicals they are using.   If they are not willing to do this
then you can only conclude that they don't have the sense to
respond to a reasonable request from a potential customer.
This would imply that they are not very serious about their
business.   You should have no further interest in such a
person.   Imagine for a moment, if they will not treat you as a
respected potential customer to your face, what they will do to
your car when you are not around.   It will probably shine, but
one would have to be VERY SUSPICIOUS about how the shine was
achieved and what the car will look like in a year or so.

Occasionally this selection procedure will eliminate someone
who actually does good work, but has a difficult time dealing
with customers.   Some professionals,   rewarded for their
technical efforts by a goodly supply of customers, become what
euphemistically is called in the trade, 'independent'.   People
where I come from would use the term 'ornery'.   Unfortunately,
unless you have some other way of determining the procedures
this person intends to use on your car, it is very difficult to
tell the difference between someone who is 'independent'   and
someone who simply is not going to do a very good job.

Given that your potential detailer will go through his/her
methods in some detail, the knowledge you have gained from this
book should allow you to quickly ascertain whether your car is
about to be well-treated or not.   Pick the best and proceed
about the other things you wish to do.   Obviously you will end
up paying good money for good service.   Keep in mind that the
detailer will be doing a complete cycle of care all at once.
Wash, wax, leather protection, etc.   This is more work than you

would likely do at any one sitting when you have the ability to schedule the tasks out, doing a little bit each time you wash the car. In California, $125 to $200 is a reasonable amount to pay, depending on the level of service, the size of the car and the current condition. Prices may range up to $400 for experts that do a very careful polishing job along with the waxing.

In the midst of all of this be a little tolerant of minor faults. While there are great rewards to seeing a car that has been in need of attention begin to really shine, detailing as a profession has some serious limitations. If you quarrel only with a procedure or two don't be afraid to ask that, in those specific cases, it be done the way you prefer.

54. The End

This is nearly the end of the book. Only the appendices remain. I hope you find that this has helped, in some small way, to guide you in useful ways of caring for your car. I also hope you enjoy your clean car and enjoy the process of keeping it that way.

APPENDIX I - Checklist for wash or wash and wax

The checklist on the next page will aid you in setting up a
smooth sequence for washing, or for washing and waxing.   You
may well find that you prefer a slightly different sequence.
This list is just to get you going.   Time for a good exterior
wash is about 25 minutes.   Another 15 minutes should get the
inside clean. Add an hour or two for the extra work to wax and
treat the exterior and interior (the interior, once clean, is
fairly easy).   Paint touch up will depend on where you and the
car have been.

CHECKLIST FOR WASH OR WASH AND WAX

For a wash-only do only the items with double asterisks. For a complete job do all items.

        Check that the door drain holes are open
    ** Vacuum inside of the car and trunk
    ** Swing mirrors toward front (Porsche)
    ** Spray 1:1 Swipe in engine compartment, in wheel wells
    ** Wipe down trunk, battery

    ** Hose off engine compartment, wheel wells, under the car
    ** Rinse the car
    ** Wash: body, wheels
    ** Rinse

    ** Remove bugs, shine chrome as needed; re-rinse
    ** Dry
        Remove water spots as needed; re-rinse, re-dry
    ** Clean the glass.

    ** Wax alloy wheels
        Wax the chrome and painted surfaces
        Treat the exterior rubber parts
    ** Spray wax or oil under the hood,
                        in the engine compartment

        Clean the carpets
    ** Wipe down the non-leather parts of the interior
    ** Wipe down the leather.
        Hide food on the Leather

        Treat the inside rubber
    ** Spray carpet with Lysol
        Wash your car cover
        Touch up paint chips as needed

APPENDIX II - BRIEF SUPPLY LIST

Purpose	Specific Product	Source	Approx. Price
General Rags	*100% cotton diapers	Toy store	$ 1.00
		Diaper Serv	$ .30
	Terrycloth towels	Automotion	$ 9.20
Easy application	*16oz spray bottles	Hardware	$ 1.39
Hold wash water	*Large wash bucket	Hardware	$ 9.99
Car wash soap	*Meguiar's 00 HighTech	Color Shop	$ 4.95/16oz
Wash the car	*Cotton wash mitt	Auto Supply	$ 2.49
Wash the wheels	*4" soft-bristle paint brush	Hardware	$ 7.49
Water Spots	*white vinegar	Supermkt	$ .49/16oz
Clean windows	*sudsy ammonia	Supermkt	$ .99/56oz
Emulsifier	*Swipe Concentrate	Smulyan	$ 8.90/qt
Solvent	*Prepsol	Color Shop	$ 9.55/gal
Vacuuming	*Wet/dry vacuum	Hardware	$59.95
	*Crevice tool	Hardware	$ 3.00
Scrubbing Carpet	*Scrubbing brush	Hardware	$ 1.79
Mild Soap	*Woolite	Supermkt	$ 1.96/16oz
Polish	*Meguiar's Deep Crystal Pol.	Auto Supply	$ 5.19/16oz
Wax Prep	*Meguiar's #7 Sealer/Resealr	Color Shop	$ 6.95/16oz
Main Wax	*Harly Carnuba	Auto Supply	$ 5.99/7oz
Remove wax	*soft toothbrush	Supermkt	$ 1.49
	*cutoff 2" paint brush (natural bristles)	Hardware	$ 3.59
Protect leather	*Hide Food - Connolly Bros.	Automotion	$ 8.50/11oz
Utility wax	*Lemon Pledge spray wax	Supermkt	$ 2.31/14oz
Protect rubber	*Meguiar's Formula 42	Color Shop	$ 7.95/16oz
	*Meguiar's Formula 40	Color Shop	$ 6.95/16oz
Oil-film	*WD-40	Auto Supply	$ 1.29/6oz.

APPENDIX III - COMPLETE SUPPLY LIST

Below you will find listed all of the recommended products and
most of those that are mentioned at all.   Asterisks indicate
critical supplies or recommended choices.

GENERAL SUPPLIES

Purpose	Specific Product	Source	Price
General Rags	100% cotton diapers	Toy store	$ 1.00
and stuff	*Used diapers	Diaper Srv	$ .30
	Terrycloth towels	Automotion	$ 9.20
	*16oz spray bottles	Hardware	$ 1.39
Tight spots	Q-tips, cotton stem	Supermkt	$ 1.47/200
Mild Soap	*Woolite	Supermkt	$ 1.96/16oz
Emulsifier	*Swipe Concentrate	Smulyan	$ 8.90/qt
	Simple Green	Hardware	$11.99/gal
	Armor All Cleaner	Hardware	$ 4.19/32oz
Solvent	*#7 Tar Remover	Hardware	$ 2.69/11oz
	*Prepsol	Color Shop	$ 9.55/gal
	Acme 88-Klix	Color Shop	
	Lacquer thinner	Hardware	
Clean windows	*sudsy ammonia	Supermkt	$ .99/56oz
Water Spots	*white vinegar	Supermkt	$ .49/16oz
Utility wax	*Lemon Pledge	Supermkt	$ 2.31/14oz
Protect rubber	*Meguiar's Form. 42	Color Shop	$ 7.95/16oz
	*Meguiar's Form. 40	Color Shop	$ 6.95/16oz
	Clean Eze	Color Shop	$12.90/gal
	303 Protectant	Auto Supply	
Oil-film	*WD-40	Auto Supply	$ 1.29/6oz.

EXTERIOR CLEANING

Purpose	Specific Product	Source	Price
Water source	*Garden hose *Sprayer *Flow nozzle		
Hold water	*Large wash bucket	Hardware	$ 9.99
Wash soap	*Meguiar's ## HighTech Meguiar's Car Wash & Conditioner Classic Car Wash	Color Shop Auto Supply	$ 4.95/16oz $ 3.19/16oz
Wash the car	*Cotton wash mitt	Auto Supply	$ 2.49
Wash wheels	*4" paint brush	Hardware	$ 7.49
Rag wringer	Dry the wiping towels		
Clean glass	Windex	Supermkt	$ 1.74/22oz
Plastic Windows	Meguiar's Mirror Glaze Plastic Cleaner Plastic Polish Eagle1 Plastic Polish	 Auto Supply Auto Supply P.B.Tweeks	 $ 4.69/8oz $ 4.69/9oz $ 3.87/12oz
Clean Chrome	Brass wool (#00, #0000)	West Marine	$ 4.29/12pads
Wheel cleaner	P21S Wheel Cleaner	P.W.Tweeks	$11.96/17oz
Polish Aluminum	Happich's Simichrome		
Battery	Permatex Battery Prot.	Auto Supply	$ 2.79/1.8oz

EXTERIOR PROTECTION

Purpose	Specific Product	Source	Price
Polish	*Meguiar's Deep Cryst.Pol.	Auto Supply	$ 5.19/16oz
	Liquid Ebony #27	Color Shop	$ 6.95/32oz
	Malm's Ultra Fine Polish	Malm's	$15.00/16oz
Wax Prep	*Meguiar's #7 Sealer and Resealer	Color Shop	$ 6.95/16oz
Main wax	Meguiar's Deep Crystal		
	Carnuba Wax(liquid)	Auto Supply	$ 5.19/16oz
	Carnuba Paste	Auto Supply	$ 4.89/12oz
	Malm's Carnuba Wax	Malm's	$15.00/16oz
	*Harly Carnuba	Auto Supply	$ 5.99/7oz
Remove wax in crevices	*soft toothbrush	Supermkt	$ 1.49
	*cutoff 2" paint brush	Hardware	$ 3.59
	half-length 1" paintbrush	Hardware	$ 1.79
Laydown Buffer	Milwaukee	Hardware	$163.99
	Black & Decker	Color Shop	$148.00
	Sears (not well balanced)	Sears	$72.00
Undercoating	Westley's Spray Underctng	Auto Supply	$ 2.99/20oz
Tire paint	Mechanic's Tire Black	Auto Supply	$ 2.19
Alloy wheels	Vaseline	Supermkt	$ 1.59/7.5oz

INTERIOR CLEANING

Vacuuming	*Wet/dry vacuum	Hardware	$59.95
	*Crevice tool	Hardware	$ 3.00
Scrub Carpet	*Scrubbing brush	Hardware	$ 1.79
Carpet Cleaners	Scotchguard Carpet Clnr	Auto Supply	$ 4.89/14oz
	Turtlewax Carpet Clnr	Auto Supply	$ 3.39/16oz
	Turtlewax Spot Remover	Auto Supply	$ 3.79/7oz

INTERIOR PROTECTION

Clean leather	Lexol cleaner	Automotion	$ 7.50/liter
Protect Leather	*Hide Food	Automotion	$ 8.50/11oz
	Lexol preservative	Automotion	$ 7.50/liter
	Leatherique Rejuvenator	Leatherique	$ 8.00/pint
Protect Uphol.	Scotchguard	Supermkt	$ 4.69/12oz
Improve smell	Spray Lysol	Hardware	$ 2.39/6oz
	Ozium new-car-smell	Auto Supply	$ 2.49

TOUCH UP

Paint	Color touch up paint	Dealer or Color Shop
	Clear touch up paint	Dealer or Color Shop

APPENDIX IV - SUPPLIERS AND BRAND NAMES.

In appendices II and III we indicated sources for the supplies. The non-mailorder supplies are shown as they are found in Northern California. I do not know how well this will be representative of product availability in other parts of the US. We are, in particular, blessed with a world-class chain of hardware stores called Orchard Supply Hardware. You may have to look in other places for some of what here shows as being available at the hardware store.

Some of the supermarket prices are actually from a deep-discount drug store.

A well-stocked color shop (supplier to body shops) will provide you with many of the products needed but not all such shops are well-stocked. The Center Paint Company in San Jose is a good example of the best of these shops. It is not a huge operation, but, as soon as you walk in the door you see just about every product that you need. They stock Prepsol, Clean Eze (which was otherwise a little hard to find) and an impressive array of Meguiar's products. They did not have the Formula 42 in stock, but had it at the store for me within 5 hours (Meguiar's delivers to their warehouse daily). They also had the Liquid Ebony.

Two of the retail auto supply chains in Northern California are Kragen's and Grand Auto. Neither had all the supplies needed, but, between the two of them, all the supplies marked 'Auto Supply' were available.

The best place I have found to get used diapers in Northern California is at Tiny Tots Diaper Service in Campbell. Their phone is 408-292-2220. They charge $3.00 for 10 diapers and have both the pre-sewn and unsewn versions.

In the process of doing this much product research I have come to have a strong respect for Meguiar's/Mirror Glaze. This company participates actively in providing products packaged

for retail stores such as Kragen's, but is on equally firm
footing in supplying the commercial users of these products
such as detailers and body shops. They seem to have a more
complete product line than anyone else. In conversations with
several of these companies, Meguiar's was shown clearly to be a
well-organized and competent company. Some of the other
companies, even some with well-recognized names, came off as
small-scale garage-level operations. Meguiar's has a very wide
range of products, just about every grade and style of cleaner,
polish, wax or other product you might need. I am NOT
suggesting that they make the best product in every category,
but I am confident that most of their products will work well.
It would take some serious scientific testing to find out which
products really are the very best.

Malm's seems to be primarily a mail-order house. They have
just a few products, but the products are very well respected.
They also have a small booklet on washing and waxing the car
that provided some useful information.

Turtle Wax, of Chicago, Illinois, markets approximately 100
products for all phases of cosmetic car care. All of their
products carry their brand name except for the Excalibur
premium waxes.

The Borden Grocery and Specialty Products Division from
Columbus, Ohio markets Rally, Rain Dance and No. 7 products.
The No. 7 products are lines that they bought from DuPont.
There are about 30 products in their catalog that are relevant
to car detailing.

Blue Coral, Inc. from Cleveland, Ohio, markets products under
the Westley's, Blue Coral, espreé, TR-3, and Mechanics brand
names. There are about 20 relevant products in their catalog.
This company also bought the Simoniz name and uses that name to
market products outside of the US. Why the Simoniz name was
discontinued within the US I do not know.

The Classic line is from the Wynn Oil company of Azusa,
California. There are only six products in this line,
a liquid car wash, an exterior cleaner and four waxes. The
Classic products I have used seem to work fine.

You may, occasionally, find products with the PRO brandname. PRO products are produced by BAF Industries, Santa Ana, California, a company that has been in business for 53 years. The company's main focus is the commercial marketplace including detailers, body shops, commercial car washes, aircraft maintenance, etc., but they have dabbled in the retail marketplace. Their Yellow Wax used to be available at Orchard Supply Hardware and is still, along with a few other products, available through some Porsche dealers. Mostly, however, you will see their name if you look around at the products being used when you visit a professional detail shop. Since it is difficult for us mortals to get our hands on these products I have made little mention of them in the body of this book.

According to Bob Moschetti, PRO sales and marketing, the company manufactures selected products for many of the companies mentioned in this book, but is not interested in seriously entering the retail market. Mr. Moschetti was also quite helpful in defining some terms and sharing some of the history of how exterior car care has changed over the years. He pointed out, quite correctly, that, whereas we used to be concerned about caring for the paint we are, these days, mostly dealing with restoring and protecting the clear coat that is over the paint on most cars.

Also according to Mr. Moschetti, PRO makes some very specialized products for treating the older lacquer paints that were common on European cars during the fifties and early sixties; P33-Troubleshooter was specifically mentioned. I am loathe to even mention this, as the product is not available through retail channels, but if you have a problem with an older European car, you may want to try to talk your friendly local detailer into getting you some of this stuff.

Listed below are the addresses and telephone numbers of the
mail-order suppliers.

Automotion   Beverly Hills Motoring Access.
3535 Kifer Road   200 South Robertson Boulevard
Santa Clara, Calif. 95051   Beverly Hills, Calif. 90211
408-736-9020   213-657-4800

Klasse Surface Protector   Leatherique Restoration Products
P.O. Box 597   369 Blanding Boulevard
Pacifica, Calif. 94044   Orange Park, Florida   32073
415-756-1911   904-276-2220

Malm's Chemical Corp.   Smulyan Distributing Company
Box 300   5872 Chesbro Avenue
Pound Ridge, NY 10576   San Jose, Calif. 95123
914-764-5775   408-227-6967

P. B. Tweeks   West Marine Products
3301 Hill Street   2450 17th Avenue
Long Beach, Calif. 90804   Santa Cruz, Calif. 95063
800-421-3776   800-538-0775
(800-782-9231 from Calif.)   (408-476-1905 from Calif.)

Appendix V - A Gasoline Story

by Garry Korpi

[This story was first printed in The Nugget, a monthly
publication of the Golden Gate Region of the Porsche
Club of America. It is reprinted here with the
permission of the author.]

The problem all started with a dirty and plugged fuel injector
in our [Porsche] 924. The available fuel at local service
stations occasionally seemed to be contaminated and I thought
that the fuel filters should be changed prior to installing the
injectors.

The 924 has one fuel filter location under the car in front of
the fuel tank. Mistake number one was to work on the fuel
system in the garage instead of in the driveway. It became
obvious that this rear filter had not been changed for some
time as I had quite a bit of trouble removing the fuel line
from the filter.

As a safety precaution, I had a plug ready for the fuel line
and a CO2 fire extinguisher on hand. Mistake number two, the
gas tank was full. Still, I knew that I had the plug for the
fuel line and figured there would be no problem. Mistake
number three, the drop light was incandescent instead of
fluorescent. This detail never entered my mind.

There I was, under the car, flat on my back, drop light next to
my head, screwdriver in hand, trying to pry off the rubber fuel
line.

I had struggled for some time with the fuel line when,
suddenly, BOOM!!, the light bulb exploded into instant flame
under the car. The fuel line had come loose and the gasoline
was pouring out. There I was, still lying on my back, under
the car, flames everywhere, including on my left arm and hand.

I said to myself, "Aw . . . . !!". At that point you have
never seen anyone move faster than 'The Kid'.

I bailed out from under the car and ran about ten feet to the
sink.   I   turned the water on full and it still took ten to
fifteen seconds to put out the flames on my arm.   Finally the
flames went out and I turned around to see flames covering the
entire underneath of the car and spreading around on the garage
floor.   Of course! All this time the fuel from the car was
feeding the flames. I grabbed the CO_2 extinguisher and almost
put out the fire until I emptied the CO_2 bottle. Then I really
had problems.   The car was really on fire,   black smoke was
choking me and completely filled the garage; (fortunately the
door was open).   The heat was intense by then and I said to
myself, "To hell with the car, save the house."

I pushed the car out of the garage and for some unknown reason
I pulled on the emergency brake half way down the driveway.   I
ran back to the garage where small fires had broken out in
several places.   I   build and fly radio-controlled model
airplanes and, of course, all the models, cans of paint, fuel,
etc. were on fire. I grabbed the garden hose and finally put
out all the small fires.   I then ran to phone the fire
department.   WRONG!!   The fire had melted the wiring and the
phones were dead. In a panic I ran next door yelling "Call the
fire department!" I hurried back to the house to find the 924
completely engulfed in flames.

Mistake number four;   the Caltrans [California Department of
Highways] pickup that I drive for work was also parked in the
drive next to the 924 and was by then also on fire. I quickly
ran back to the house to get the keys to the truck but the
front door was locked. So I dashed back through the smokey
garage and opened the door to the house. This maneuver, of
course, let all the smoke pour into the house. I retrieved the
keys, moved the pickup, grabbed the hose and put out the truck
fire.   In the meantime the 924 was burning furiously with
flames about 15 to 20 feet in the air and no sign of the fire
department.

At that point I remembered the animals. I dashed back into the house, scared the hell out of the cats, grabbed the dogs and ran back outside again.   With all the noise and activity quite a crowd of curious neighbors had gathered.   I handed the dogs to one of the neighbors and just at that point the fire department arrived.   OOPS!   They had sent a small truck designed to put out small grass fires with water only.   The driver said, "Can't use water on a gasoline fire, I'll send for another truck."   (I didn't have the heart to tell him that I had just put out the pickup fire with my "little ole garden hose.")

About this time I realized that the 924 was a total,   so I decided I needed pictures of the event.   I went back to the house, got the camera and started clicking away.   Finally the fire department arrived with a hook and ladder truck.   I told the fellows "Don't try very hard to put out the fire on the 924,   I   think it's gone."   Suddenly two loud explosions occurred.   No,   it wasn't the gas tank, it was the shock absorbers which sounded like mortar shells as they exploded. One fired fifty feet back into the garage, through the cupboard door and into a case of cat food. What next?!!

More small fires had broken out in the garage.   They were caused by the model fuels and were burning merrily. About then the paramedics arrived. I don't know why, no one was hurt. At least not me. Wrong. The initial shock was wearing off and I suddenly realized that my arm hurt like the devil.   I looked down to see skin dripping down and mixing with the sleeve of my coveralls.

The paramedics convinced me to go to the hospital,   but not until I left instructions with the fire department and neighbors on how to handle things.   Great help, GARRY! On the way to the hospital the arm really hurt and the paramedics used almost six quarts of ice water to cool it.

At emergency I pleaded for some pain pills or a shot.   I finally got the shot which made me forget the arm, as the shot hurt worse.   The nurse asked me if I wanted to notify anyone, like my wife Sheila, maybe.   I said, "Sure, but tell her I'm okay and just come pick me up."

The nurse called and left a message that I needed to be picked up.   Sheila received the message,   immediately left work and stopped by the house to get directions to the hospital.   After seeing the burned out hulk of the car and the condition of the house she had serious doubts as to how "okay" Garry was.

In the end everything turned out fine.   After three months of hassle with the insurance companies the house was repaired and we purchased a new 1983 Porsche 944.

I did learn some important lessons, though. Do not work on the auto fuel system in the garage, or with a full fuel tank. Never use a drop light with an incandescent bulb.   Be sure you have replacement value on all insured items.   Pictures or videos of all your belongings will also help save lots of hassles later.